THE GOD OF GREAT REVERSALS

THE GOD OF GREAT REVERSALS

THE GOSPEL IN THE
BOOK OF ESTHER

Timothy Cain

ISBN-13: 978-1796316315

Cover Design: Gabriel Leake
Editing and Typesetting: Charity Edwards

Printed in the Unites States of America

To Tayla, my precious daughter.

Never forget that you too have been loved by a King.

CONTENTS

Acknowledgements   3

Introduction   5

1. Opening Act   11

2. Compromise   25

3. Beauty   43

4. Cliffhanger   59

5. Devastation   77

6. Providence   93

7. Life & Death   113

8. Pride   125

9. Intercession   139

10. Great Reversals   155

Appendix: Holy War   171

ACKNOWLEDGEMENTS

This book began as a sermon series at Kaleo Church in the spring of 2014. I will never get over the privilege that it is to be able to study God's Word and proclaim it to His people each week. Thank you to Kaleo Church for your love for the Gospel and the anticipation with which you come back week after week to hear more about our great God.

While I have always wanted to turn a sermon series into a book, I never knew if it would really happen. And now after seeing how much work actually goes into it, I can't believe that it ever did. It all started when I found out that Charity Edwards had a B.A. in English and enjoyed editing things. One Saturday night after church, I asked her if she would ever consider editing some sermon manuscripts for me in the hopes of putting together a book. Charity liked the idea, and we picked the book of Esther as a great place to start. I don't think either one of us knew what we were getting into. That was over a year ago, and I cannot imagine how many hours Charity has put into editing since then. Without Charity, this book would have never been more than a dream. Charity, thank you, thank you for the countless hours you put into editing the manuscripts and making this dream a reality. I would have given up long ago without your help.

I want to thank my mom who has been faithfully praying for me since I was little. She also spent many hours editing the manuscripts and has been a great encouragement throughout this entire process. Mom, I love you. Thank you for your persistent prayers; I shudder to think of where I would be without them.

I want to thank my wife Abbey who has been by my side throughout this entire process. Abbey, you are precious gift of God, and I am so thankful that we get to make this pilgrimage together.

Lastly, I want to thank my precious Savior Jesus Christ. What a tragedy my life would be without You. Thank You for leaving the comforts of heaven and coming to earth to be the man that I have failed to be. Thank You for taking all of my sin and bearing it in Your body on the cross. You bravely went before the King on my behalf even though You knew it would cost You dearly. As George Herbert once said, "Thou art my loveliness, my life, my light, beauty alone to me."

INTRODUCTION

HAVE YOU EVER read the Bible and come away feeling distant, like the world described there was so different from your world that you found it hard to relate to? We read Exodus, about how the people witness the ten plagues and see the Red Sea part and eat manna in the desert, and we think, "If I were in their shoes, of course I would follow God." We think, "If I looked out my window and there was a huge cloud that sat over the church building and talked to the pastor whenever he went into his office, then I would find it pretty easy to follow God and even listen to my pastor."

All throughout the Bible, there seem to be miracles and the audible voice of God. He speaks to His prophets, then the prophets speak to the people, and everything they say ends up coming true. Then Jesus comes and does miracle after miracle— healing people and feeding massive crowds and raising people from the dead. Even after Jesus returns to heaven, the Holy Spirit visibly comes down and rests on people, and the apostles do miracles and cast out demons and heal people. When you read these things, it makes you wonder how anyone failed to believe in God when He seemed so obviously present.

But in our world, things don't seem to work like this, do they? In our world:

- If you want to eat, you have to get up, go to work, get paid, go to the store, and buy your food.

Introduction

- You don't see many miracles, and you don't hear many voices from heaven. Most of the people who say they hear voices from heaven aren't nearly as reliable as the Old Testament prophets.
- Our bosses seem to exercise more control over our lives than God does.
- Our lives are often more affected by what a girl or guy thinks about us than they are by what God thinks.
- Most of us find it really hard to see exactly where God is or what He is up to.
- Things like money and approval seem to hold the keys to success and happiness.

It's easy to wonder, "If God is real, then why doesn't He make Himself more clear? If God wants us to believe in Him, then why doesn't He make it easier for us to see Him?" We want to know why God doesn't do more things like He did back in the Bible times.

If you have ever felt this way, welcome to the book of Esther. In this book, all of God's promises are threatened, and His people find themselves on the brink of extinction. If ever there were a time for God to show Himself, this would seem to be it. And yet:

- God's name isn't even mentioned.
- There are no visions or directions from God about how to avoid disaster.
- There are no miracles, and God never supernaturally shows up to rescue His people from their enemies.

Instead, the book of Esther reads a lot like the story of our lives. God's people are living as foreigners in a pagan culture that doesn't share their beliefs about God. They are surrounded by a society that judges everything by appearances and is constantly trying to seduce them into seeking satisfaction in the temporary pleasures of this world. As the story unfolds, the culture grows hostile towards God's people; before you know it, they find themselves in grave danger. All the while, the God of the Bible seems strangely silent.

In the book of Daniel, God appears miraculously to His people in exile to prove that He is real; but in the book of Esther, God remains hidden behind the scenes. In the book of Esther, if God's people are going to avoid compromise and continue to follow God, it's not going to be because He supernaturally shows up. If God's people are going to remain faithful, they are going to have to look back in history and trust that the God Who had delivered His people in the past will deliver them again. They will have to trust that even though they don't see God, He is there; that even though they have no idea what He is doing, they can know for certain that He will not fail to keep any of His promises.

Now how familiar does that sound? This is a book that we can relate to, isn't it? You and I find ourselves living in a culture that doesn't believe what we believe. Just like in Esther's day, our culture is:

- calling us to pursue its definition of success.
- telling us to abandon the God we can't see and seek our satisfaction in the things of this world.

- urging us to compromise our beliefs so that we can all live together peaceably.
- growing more and more hostile to the claims of absolute truth.

And it's hard to resist, isn't it? It's hard to resist, because the things our culture promises seem so tangible, while the promises of God often seem so far away. Often we wish that God would simply show Himself, that He would prove that He is real, that He would do something like He did in the Bible so that we might find it easier to believe in Him.

But He doesn't usually do that. Instead, just as He did in Esther's day, our God calls us to remember all that He has done for us already. He calls us to remember everything that He accomplished for us through the life and death and resurrection of His son, Jesus—and, based on that, to trust Him. Our God is calling us to believe that even when we don't see Him, the God Who did not spare His only Son is at work, and He will keep all His promises.

That is where the book of Esther comes in. It comes to us right where we are and calls us not to give in to the seductive voices of our culture. It calls us to trust that our God is at work even when we don't see Him.

The book is going to do that in at least three ways. It will:

1. expose the foolishness of pursuing the things of this world.
2. show us that God is at work keeping His promises even when we don't see Him.

3. show us that as beautiful and alluring as the things of this
    world might seem, Jesus is even better.

So let's dive in.

CHAPTER 1: OPENING ACT

Text: Esther 1

Now in the days of Ahasuerus, the Ahasuerus who reigned from India to Ethiopia over 127 provinces, in those days when King Ahasuerus sat on his royal throne in Susa, the citadel, in the third year of his reign he gave a feast for all his officials and servants. The army of Persia and Media and the nobles and governors of the provinces were before him, while he showed the riches of his royal glory and the splendor and pomp of his greatness for many days, 180 days. And when these days were completed, the king gave for all the people present in Susa the citadel, both great and small, a feast lasting for seven days in the court of the garden of the king's palace.

(Esther 1:1-6)

THE BOOK OF Esther begins by giving us a picture of a man who has "arrived," so to speak. Verse 1:1 says, "Now in the days of Ahasuerus, the Ahasuerus who reigned from India to Ethiopia over 127 provinces . . ." You are supposed to be impressed. Ahasuerus is the most powerful man in the entire world.

After taking two years to consolidate his empire, King Ahasuerus has gathered the military and nobles and leaders and is throwing them a massive party. Verse 4 explains why: "to show them the riches of his royal glory and the splendor and pomp of his greatness . . ." In other words, the king has achieved everything this world has to offer, so he throws a huge party.

Now just to give you a hint about how wealthy this king is, it takes him 180 days to parade all of his wealth before the people (Esther 1:4). Think about that. There used to be a show called "Cribs" where a celebrity would take one hour just to show off how amazing his or her house was. That is what this king does—except for him, the show takes 180 days and includes a complimentary feast for viewers.

THEN, just in case the people aren't impressed by the 180-day feast where he has shown off all his stuff, the king throws another feast right afterwards for seven days—and this time he shows off his generosity by inviting the entire city (Esther 1:5).

We don't have categories for how rich and powerful this king was. Verses 6 and 7 describe the scene:

> There were white cotton curtains and violet hangings fastened with cords of fine linen and purple to silver rods and marble pillars, and also couches of gold and silver on a mosaic pavement of porphyry, marble, mother-of-pearl and precious stones.

They put pearls and precious stones in the floor! Imagine the scene with the builders:

> Builders: Oh great king, what type of floor would you like for your palace?
>
> King: I don't know, you know that room full of pearls and diamonds and rubies and sapphire? Why don't you throw some of those in the floor so that it sparkles in the light.

I heard of a rapper who made his dog a $75,000 platinum and ruby collar, and people thought he was a bit excessive. Well, this king walks on rubies! $75,000 would buy a slab of his floor. Some people think leather couches are nice, but this guy makes them out of gold. He even drinks from cups made out of gold.

There are only two other places in the Old Testament that are described in as much glorious detail as this king's palace: the temple and the tabernacle. At the time of Esther's story, the tabernacle is long gone, the temple has been burned, and God is seemingly nowhere to be found. From the outside, it looks like the king is the one with all the wealth and glory.

In verse 8, we find that the king loves not just wealth and pleasure, but also power. Notice everything that takes place at the party must be under his control. The king even makes a law about how much people can drink! Fortunately for the party guests, the law states that, "there is no compulsion." So people can drink as they please.

Opening Act

This is the world that the king holds out to his people in the hopes of impressing them. The king is parading all of his splendor before the people, hoping that they will be impressed and want to be more like him. He is hoping they will value what he values and will join him in seeking satisfaction in the things of this world.

Not a lot has changed, has it? If this party were going on right now, do you think there would be news cameras there? Do you think there might be a show about it? Do you think anyone would be interested? If this party were going on right now, I bet it would make for the biggest reality show ever.

Our culture loves the same things that the Persians loved: wealth, power, pleasure, comfort, control. Just as it did in Esther's day, our culture is constantly calling us to embrace their values; if we are honest, we have to admit that often we give in.

Think about it: have you ever tried to impress anyone before? Ever exaggerate a story, show off a skill, or gossip about someone else in order to appear in a better light?

Have you ever looked at something and thought, "If only I had that, then I would be happy"? It doesn't matter what it is. For some of you, it's a certain look or certain hair or a certain body. For some of you, it's a certain type of home or a certain job or a certain relationship. For others, it's simply the respect or approval of a certain person. While none of us thinks we need as much as the king has, each of us has certain things that we think would complete our lives.

The world wants you to give your life to trying to get what the king has. The world calls you to do whatever it takes to become more like the king. But the book of Esther comes to unmask the façade and show us the truth.

On the last day of the feast, the king is drunk, and he commands seven of his servants to go and get his wife (Esther 1:10-11). It is the last day of the feast, and the king wants to show off to all his guests his most prized possession. So he calls for his beautiful wife. He's thinking, "Anyone who hasn't been impressed with the last 187 days will be surely be impressed when they see how beautiful my wife is!"

The world calls you to do whatever it takes to become more like the king. But the book of Esther comes to unmask the façade and show us the truth.

But then look at what verse 12 says: "But Queen Vashti refused to come at the king's command. . ." This is meant to blow you away. For 187 days, the king has been trying to impress people by showing them just how rich and powerful he is; but as the feast comes to a close, all anyone is going to remember is that his wife refused his command.

His wife isn't impressed. She sees beneath the surface, and she isn't fooled. All of a sudden, the king doesn't look nearly as powerful as he once did. The king who rules over 127 provinces from India to Ethiopia can't even control his own wife. Verse 12 says, "At this the king became enraged, and his anger burned within him."

The richest most powerful man in the world who has everything you could ever wish for comes to the end of 187 days of partying and feasting, and he is angry.

Now notice what happens next. Instead of realizing that he shouldn't have tried to use his wife and letting the matter go, the king turns her refusal into a matter of national security. In his anger, the king gathers his seven top advisors to help him figure out what he should do. One of the men, named Memucan, steps up and says,

> "Not only against the king has Queen Vashti done wrong, but also against all the officials and all the peoples who are in all the provinces of King Ahasuerus. For the queen's behavior will be made known to all women, causing them to look at their husbands with contempt. . ." (Esther 1:16-18)

Notice how the problem is blown out of all proportion. This guy thinks that Vashti's refusing to come to the king could threaten the very fabric of their society. If something drastic isn't done, no wife will ever listen to her husband again!

So what does Memucan propose? In verse 19, he says,

> "If it please the king, let a royal order go out from him, and let it be written among the laws of the Persians and the Medes so that it may not be repealed, that Vashti is never again to come before king Ahasuerus. And let the king give her royal position to another who is better than she. So when the decree made by the king is proclaimed throughout all his kingdom, for it is vast, all women will give honor to their husbands, high and low alike."

This command is funny on at least three levels:

1. Memucan is like, "If we don't do something, everyone is going to hear about this." So what does he do? He makes a law that is translated into every single language of the empire so that now everyone really will hear about this embarrassing situation.
2. Vashti's punishment is not being able to see the face of the king—which is what she wanted in the first place.
3. Memucan thinks that he can legislate that wives need to honor their husbands. He thinks that the key to getting people's respect is making a law.

Despite all of this, the advice pleases the king, and letters are sent to every province under his reign (Esther 1:21-22).

Suddenly all the greatness of the king seems to be paper thin, doesn't it? Yes, he might be king, but his own wife won't listen to him. Yes, he may throw a party that lasts 187 days, but it doesn't make him happy. Yes, the laws of the Medes and Persians might never be able to be repealed, but they are written by drunk advisors who think that they can make their wives respect them by making a law about it.

Now that we have looked at this part of the story, I want to highlight a few things that we can learn from it.

THE BOOK OF ESTHER EXPOSES THE FOOLISHNESS OF PURSUING THE THINGS OF THIS WORLD.

This story makes it radically clear that the things of this world are not big enough to satisfy us. The king throws a 187-day party, and when it ends, he isn't even happy. If a 187-day party that parades all of your extravagant possessions in front of the most important people in the world can't satisfy, then why do you think what you are looking for will satisfy? Do you really think that:

- the relationship you are after will satisfy you?
- a different job will make you happy?
- having kids will fulfill your life?
- owning your own house will make you content?
- being able to impress a certain person will bring joy?
- getting just the right grades will make your problems go away?

It won't. I am telling you: it won't. The world can't keep its promises. No matter how good something looks, it will never be enough.

Do you want to know why the king was trying so hard to impress people? It was because he was getting ready to go to war with the Greeks, and he wanted to inspire the army to join him. You see, even with everything that King Ahasuerus had, it wasn't enough. His 127 provinces weren't enough. His 187-day feast wasn't enough. If even King Ahasuerus thought he needed more, you can know for certain that nothing in this world will ever be enough to satisfy you and me.

THE BOOK OF ESTHER SHOWS THAT GOD KEEPS HIS PROMISES EVEN WHEN WE DON'T SEE HIM.

This story shows us that sometimes we have to wait to see what God is doing. Notice that God doesn't seem to be present anywhere in this story. A drunk king parades his wealth and then deposes his queen for refusing to appear before him. Where is God in that? In fact, I have a question for you: how do you think you would react if that happened in our country today?

What if the President of the United States took six months off and used tax dollars to throw himself a huge party with all his friends? And then at the end he got drunk and divorced his wife and made a law that all wives needed to honor their husbands? I can assure you that Fox News would be going crazy. Christians all over the country would be thinking that God had abandoned them. They would probably think the world was coming to an end, and some would think that God was judging the country for taking prayer out of schools all those years ago.

This is pretty much what happens in the book of Esther, and the author isn't scared. He isn't scared because he believes that God is in control. He believes that even when you can't see what God is doing, He is still at work. He believes that—come what may—God is going to keep His promises. That is why he isn't scared.

And do you know what? He is right. What happens in chapter 1 sets in motion a chain of events that will ultimately result in the deliverance of God's people. God is at work, and God will keep His promises.

Think about it: If there were no feast, there would be no drunk king; no drunk king, no call to his wife; no call to his wife, no refusal; no refusal, no angry king; no angry king, no foolish counsel; no foolish counsel, no Vashti deposal; no Vashti deposal, no Esther; no Esther, no Jews; no Jews, no Jesus; no Jesus, no hope.

God was at work then, and He is at work now—even with all the political instability, even with all the fear rhetoric that we hear on the news. With all the crazy things that happen that make it really hard to know what God is doing, we need to be reminded of the book of Esther.

God is in control, God is at work, and God will keep his promises. No recession, no dictator, no terrorist, no natural disaster will ever be able to thwart God's promises to His people. So whatever may be going on in your life or in this world, you don't have to be afraid.

THE BOOK OF ESTHER REMINDS US THAT AS BEAUTIFUL AND ALLURING AS THE THINGS OF THIS WORLD MIGHT SEEM, JESUS IS BETTER.

This story about a king calling for his bride to come to a feast is actually set in the context of a bigger story, about another King who calls His bride to come to a feast. The Bible tells us that Jesus is the true King, the king of Kings, and His people are His bride.

Even though Jesus is a King, He isn't like Ahasuerus. King Ahasuerus sent seven servants to get his wife so that he could parade her around as a sex object before a crowd of drunken men. This king cared nothing for his wife. This king was willing to expose her to shame in order to impress his friends. And when she refused to come, this king sent her away, never to see his face again.

In contrast, Jesus didn't send His servants to call His bride; instead, He left heaven and took on flesh and came to call her Himself. Even though He came to His own people, John 1:11 tells us that His own people did not receive Him. Even though He had made His people, even though He had given them life, even though He offered them Himself, His own people did not receive Him.

As the King, He should have banished us. That is what the law would have had Him do. The law would say that the wages of sin is death (Romans 6:23) and that everyone who has sinned against this King should perish in hell, never to see His face again. That is the punishment that every one of us deserves.

Jesus didn't send His servants to call His bride; instead, He left heaven and took on flesh and came to call her Himself.

But that's not what this King did. Instead of banishing His people like Ahasuerus did, Jesus chose to take the punishment of His people upon Himself. Instead of forsaking us like we deserved, Jesus went to the cross and endured the wrath we deserved from God the Father.

He literally took our punishment for us. That is what Hebrews 13:12 is talking about when it says, "So Jesus also suffered outside the gate in order to sanctify the people through his own blood." He suffered outside the gate, He took our banishment, He died our death, and He was forsaken by the Father so that He would not have to turn His face away from us.

And now this Jesus comes to invite you and me to a feast—one unlike any feast this world has ever seen. Read what Isaiah 25:6-8 says about this feast:

> On this mountain, the LORD of hosts will make for all peoples a feast of rich food, a feast of well-aged wine, of rich food full of marrow, of aged wine well refined. And he will swallow up on this mountain the covering that is cast over all peoples, the veil that is spread over all nations. He will swallow up death forever; and the LORD God will wipe away tears from all faces, and the reproach of his people he will take away from all the earth, for the LORD has spoken.

The imagery of this verse is powerful. This world has a lot of amazing things that it can offer. In fact, the first few verses of Esther reveal just how much this world has to offer. The world can give you rich food and well-aged wine. But the Isaiah passage above tells us that there is a covering that is cast over all people, a veil that we can't take off—and that veil is death.

What this means is that everything amazing that this world has to offer must always be experienced through the veil of death. The pleasures, the joys, the relationships—everything—can only be experienced through the veil of death. No matter how much you enjoy them, you know they won't last. All the money and power in this world can't remove the veil.

But look at Isaiah 25:7-8: "And He will swallow up on this mountain the covering that is cast over all peoples, the veil that is spread over all nations. He will swallow up death forever . . ." That is our king! He is the one Who has swallowed death for us.

On that mountain, Jesus died the death we deserved. He rose again from the dead, and He has swallowed death forever. And now He comes to invite us to a feast—a feast that we can enjoy without the veil, a feast that will last forever.

THIS is the feast you want to go to—the feast where the groom will lift up your veil and wipe away every tear. At that wedding, you will not have to say, "'Til death do us part," because you will see the nail scars on His hands reminding you that He has swallowed death forever.

So don't be like Vashti. Your King is nothing like her king, so you don't have to refuse like she did. Your King is here, and He is inviting you to come to Him and live, to come to Him and have your sins forgiven, to come to Him and experience the life you have always longed for. In His presence is the fullness of joy, and at His right hand are pleasures forevermore (Psalm 16:11), pleasures that you can enjoy without the veil of death hanging over you.

Won't you get up from the table of this world and follow Jesus? Won't you forsake the passing pleasures of this world in order to enjoy the eternity you were made for? Your Savior has invited you to a feast. Won't you accept His invitation?

Chapter 2: Compromise

Text: Esther 2

After these things, when the anger of King
Ahasuerus had abated, he remembered Vashti
and what she had done and what had been
decreed against her. Then the king's young men
who attended him said, "Let beautiful young
virgins be sought out for the king. And let the
king appoint officers in all the provinces of his
kingdom to gather all the beautiful young virgins
to the harem in Susa the capital, under custody
of Hegai, the king's eunuch, who is in charge of
the women. Let their cosmetics be given them.
And let the young woman who pleases the king
be queen instead of Vashti." This pleased the
king, and he did so.

(Esther 2:1-4)

I MAGINE WITH ME, what it would be like to watch this story
on a movie screen.

The camera begins with a wide angle, and you are blown away
by the wealth and beauty of this ancient city. As the camera

zooms in, you see a palace full of people feasting. You hear laughing and shouting. The crowd is reclined on couches made out of gold and silver. The floors shimmer and shine in the sunlight because they are full of diamonds and rubies and other precious stones that reflect the light. At the head table reclines the most powerful man in all the world. He rules over an empire that stretches from India to Persia, and he is throwing a party that exceeds anything you could imagine. On the bottom of the screen, the caption: "On the 187th day of the feast."

The king summons seven eunuchs and dispatches them. The voice-over narrator tells us that the king is drunk and he is calling the queen, "in order to show the peoples and the princes her beauty, for she was lovely to look at" (Esther 2:11).

A few minutes later, you see the seven eunuchs return—without the king's wife. Jaws drop; no one can believe what is happening. The king who has spent a small fortune trying to impress people realizes that he is losing control, and he gathers his advisers to see what to do. At their advice, the king decides to make a law that will be sent to every city in his empire: the queen is never to see his face again. He hopes that this law will make women everywhere have a newfound respect for their husbands.

Now most scholars believe that the next thing the king does is raise up a massive army meant to expand his empire by going to war with the Greeks. (One of the battles of this war was made popular by the movie 300.) However, the king loses this war and returns after two years, defeated and humiliated.

So here is this man who looks like he has everything, but all he can think about right now is what he doesn't have. Esther 2:1

says, "He remembered Vashti and what she had done and what had been decreed against her."

Some of the young men around the king see the way he is feeling, and they come up with a plan. They put their heads together and come up with something they think will do the trick. They say to the king, "King, we think we know what you need. You need a bunch of beautiful, young virgins! So why don't you send out all of your officers over your entire empire and have them find all the beautiful young virgins and bring them to you. And then we will clean them up and give them make-up, and you can sleep with them one at a time. When you find the woman that pleases you, she can be queen instead of Vashti." No one should be surprised that this idea pleases the king.

The camera switches scenes to a small home just across town. Verse 5 says, "Now there was a Jew in Susa . . ." Notice the first thing the author wants us to know about this man is that he is a Jew. We don't even know his name yet. Later we find out his name is Mordecai and that he is from the tribe of Benjamin. His family was carried away in the exile when Nebuchadnezzar came and took them captive.

Over 40 years earlier, Cyrus had issued a decree that allowed all the Jews to return to their homeland. Some Jews decided to return to Jerusalem and rebuild the temple and the walls; we read about these people in the books of Ezra and Nehemiah. However, many Jews found themselves comfortable where they were and so chose not to return home. Mordecai is one of the Jews who has grown comfortable in Susa and has chosen not to return to Jerusalem.

Compromise

Of course, Cyrus's decree put these Jews in a very difficult situation. Every day, these Jews were faced with the question, "How will we keep our faith in God while trying to be successful in a culture that doesn't share our beliefs?" This is one of the key themes in the book of Esther. How does someone maintain their faith in a culture that doesn't worship the true God?

In verse 7, we find out that Mordecai isn't living alone:

> He was bringing up Hadassah, that is Esther, the daughter of his uncle, for she had neither father nor mother. The young woman had a beautiful figure and was lovely to look at, and when her father and her mother died, Mordecai took her as his own daughter.

Notice the author introduces Esther as a beautiful Jewish girl with two names. Esther is the only character in this book introduced with two names. Many people think that the author is trying to depict Esther as a young woman trying to live in two different worlds. Part of her is Hadassah, the Jewish woman who worships Yahweh, the Creator of heaven and earth; the other part of her is Esther, the beautiful young woman trying to make it in a world that only cares about her appearance.

Having heard about how beautiful Esther is, we should not be surprised at all when we come to verse 8 and realize that

> . . . when the king's order and his edict were proclaimed, and when many young women were gathered in Susa the citadel in custody of Hegai, Esther also was taken into the

king's palace and put in custody of Hegai, who had charge of the women.

Notice the passive verb: Esther "was taken." This implies that she finds herself swept along by circumstances that are outside of her control. One minute, she is a young woman named Hadassah growing up in a Jewish home surrounded by a pagan society. The next minute, she is ripped away from her home and her family and thrown into the very heart of this pagan empire where her only hope of survival seems to be for her to become Esther.

And that is exactly what she does. Verse 9 says, "And the young woman pleased him and won his favor." Esther wins the favor of Hegai by completely throwing herself into the world of the palace. How does she do that? Verse 10 tells us, "Esther had not made known her people or kindred, for Mordecai had commanded her not to make it known." One commentator says, "Esther's enviable progress in one world, the world of the empire of Ahasuerus, came at the cost of completely suppressing her identity as a citizen of the kingdom of God."[1]

I want you to notice the subtlety of the temptation that Esther gives in to. She doesn't deny her faith—she simply conceals it. And she isn't alone. It is Mordecai who tells her that she needs to conceal her faith. Why? Because he is worried about her and he wants to protect her. Verse 10 tells us that every single day, he walks in front of the gate near the harem to find out how Esther is doing. Mordecai must believe that if she were to be bold about

---

[1] Ian M. Duguid, *Esther and Ruth* (Phillipsburg: P&R Publishing, 2005), 27.

her faith, she would be discriminated against, and he doesn't want his little girl to suffer. It works. By concealing her faith and embracing the values of the empire, Esther wins the favor of Hegai and is immediately given special privileges.

Now the author decides to take a moment to explain the rules of this competition. Basically what happens is that each young woman has to go through a one-year beautifying regimen to get ready for her one night with the king. When that special night comes for one of the young women, she gets to bring whatever she wants from the harem with her into the king's chamber. In the evening, she goes in, and in the morning she leaves and is transferred to another harem under a different eunuch (more about this later).

For now what you need to know is that Esther buys it. She knows the rules and decides to use them to her advantage. She conceals her faith and wins the favor of the people in charge of the competition. In verse 15, the author tells us that Esther is, ". . . winning favor in the eyes of all who saw her."

Notice that she has molded herself into the image of the empire. How does she win favor with *everyone*? Through her looks. Esther has embraced the values of the empire, and she has excelled more than any of the other women in becoming what the king is looking for. When it's finally her turn to go into the king, she uses this favor to her advantage. She asks the man who is in charge of the whole event what she should bring in with her for her one night, and she only brings in what he advises her to.

And so it is that when Esther's night with the king comes,

... in the seventh year of his reign, the king loved Esther more than all the women, and she won grace and favor in his sight more than all the virgins, so he set the royal crown on her head and made her queen instead of Vashti. (Esther 2:17)

Esther wins! By concealing her faith and embracing the values of the empire, Esther becomes exactly what this pagan king is looking for in a wife.

I want you to notice something. I want you to notice that God is nowhere to be found in this story. Yet His absence isn't conspicuous.

Let me explain. My wife Abbey and I are hoping to adopt a child from Africa, and one of the things we had to do was take a class called "Conspicuous Adoption." This class was all about adoptions that are obviously noticeable just by appearance. Right now when Abbey and I go somewhere and people see our family for the first time, very few people would ever guess that my daughter Tayla was adopted—it's just not really noticeable from the outside. But if God gives us a child from Africa, then whenever people look at our family, they will know that we have adopted. That is what a conspicuous adoption is.

Well, in this passage, God isn't mentioned, but His absence isn't conspicuous; it's not really noticeable. The story makes complete sense just the way it is. There is not a place where the character is counting on God to show up, and then God doesn't. That would be conspicuous. But in this story, God doesn't show up, and everything still works out just fine.

Compromise

No one in this story is really expecting God to show up anyway. Esther and Mordecai have a plan to be successful, and their plan doesn't include God because they aren't very confident that He will show up.

Isaiah 30:1 talks about what this looks like. God says, "'Ah, stubborn children . . . who carry out a plan, but not mine, and who make an alliance, but not of my Spirit . . . .'" Esther and Mordecai come up with a plan, but it isn't a plan that depends upon God. Esther makes an alliance, but it is with Hegai instead of with Yahweh.

I get it. I know that many of you may think I am being a little too hard on Esther. Some of you may even be offended that someone would question the character of this woman who has a book of the Bible named after her.

Others of you may be willing to admit that Esther probably is compromising; but honestly, what choice does she have? I mean seriously, what is the alternative? All Esther is doing is trying to make the best out of a horrible situation. All you have to do is consider her three alternatives to realize just how difficult her situation is:

1. *Foregoing Hospitality.* Is Esther really supposed to tell Hegai on the first day that she gets there, "You know what? I know I am new here and should just be grateful, but I can't eat your food because my God calls it unclean, so I have put together a little list and thought maybe you could have a special diet made up just for me. Thanks for understanding"?

2. *Foregoing the King's Request.* When Esther's big night finally comes, is she really supposed to tell the king (whose character we have already seen), "Your Majesty, I know that you have spent tons of money putting me through a whole year of beautifying treatment and I am not going to lie—it has worked really well, and I do look pretty amazing. But I believe that my husband is the only one who should ever see me without my clothes on, and my God has asked me not to have sex with anyone until I am married. So I don't mind spending the night with you, but I was thinking maybe we could sit on your gold couch and talk and tell stories and just kind of get to know each other a little bit. What would you think about that?"

3. *Foregoing Honor.* Even if the king goes along with these first two things, what is she supposed to tell him after he loves her and chooses to make her the queen? Is she really supposed to tell him, "You know King, I appreciate the gesture so much, and you have been so gracious to me, but because I am a Jew, I am not allowed to marry an uncircumcised Gentile who doesn't worship the true God. I am so sorry, king, but I have to put God first"?[2]

If that is what not-compromising looks like, then who can blame Esther? I mean, you can see the dilemma that Esther faced. There is no easy answer. There is simply no convenient way for Esther to avoid compromise.

---

[2] In Jerusalem, only a little while after this takes place, we see Ezra appalled at the faithlessness of God's people in choosing to marry foreigners (Ezra 9).

Compromise

Obviously, Esther may wish that she could have stayed Hadassah and had a normal life worshiping God, but that choice isn't on the table. Instead, Esther has to choose between putting God first and opening herself up to whatever suffering that may come with it, or concealing her identity and trying to make the best of a difficult situation, hoping that maybe God will understand.

That is the difficult choice that Esther finds herself facing. And yet, as hard as it might seem, the truth is that Esther does have a choice. It wasn't too long before this that Daniel and his three friends found themselves in a similar situation—though they chose to handle it very differently.

Daniel 1:8 says,

> But Daniel resolved that he would not defile himself with the king's food, or with the wine that he drank. Therefore he asked the chief of the eunuchs to allow him not to defile himself. And God gave Daniel favor and compassion in the sight of the chief of the eunuchs . . .

Notice this text talks about God. Daniel didn't win this guy's favor like Esther did; God gave it to him because Daniel threw himself on the mercy of God. Daniel lived in such a way that if God didn't show up, he would have been undone. Daniel chose to put God first, and he was willing to suffer whatever consequences might come with that.

APPLICATION

I remember the heaviest elders meeting I ever sat in. Missionaries in Islamic countries were asking the elders how they were supposed to counsel Muslims who converted to Christianity. Other missionaries were telling their converts that they should be secret Christians. Instead of telling their families they were Christian and then being ostracized and sometimes beaten and killed, these converts were being told they could conceal their new faith. They could go to the mosque and do everything their Muslim family did; only they would be praying to Jesus instead of to Allah.

The missionaries of the church I was at wanted to know what they should tell their converts. Was it okay for them to conceal their faith and keep their families like Esther did, or should they tell them to acknowledge their faith and be baptized and face whatever consequences came with that like Daniel did?

It was over much prayer and many tears that the elders decided that it is not okay to conceal your faith. It is not okay to be a secret Christian, even if it costs you your life. The elders wanted the missionaries to tell their converts that Jesus is worth it, and that they should be faithful unto death. I will never forget how heavy that night felt. We knew that men and women would likely die because of the decision that was made there.

I will never forget going home and sitting in my room and thinking about compromise. I realized that night just how much I had compromised even though my life had never been threatened. I realized that even though the suffering I would experience for my faith was small compared to theirs, I'd often chosen to live like Esther. I looked at my life and realized how inconspicuous God's absence often was. I realized how often I have a plan that I think will work whether or not God shows up.

Let's ask ourselves these questions:

- How many of us are living in such dependence upon God that if He didn't keep His promises, we would be undone?
- How many of us, like Esther, have concealed our faith in order to avoid being uncomfortable?
- How many of us have bought into the values of this world and allowed ourselves to get caught up and carried along by them instead of putting God first in our lives?

A few months after that elder meeting, one of the missionaries sent the elders a letter he had just received. It was written by a woman in the Middle East, and she told them that her sister had become a Christian; when her sister told her about her faith, she had begged her sister not to tell anyone else. She pled with her sister to keep her faith a secret. But her sister wouldn't listen. Her sister told her family, and this woman watched as her family took her sister outside into the streets and beat her and kicked her until she was dead.

This woman watched her sister die. She wrote, "as I watched her out there in the street I saw a peace in her eyes that I know I have never experienced. And I knew in that moment that Jesus was real and that He was the one I had been looking for." This woman ran away and emailed one of the missionaries to tell them that she was now a Christian, and she wanted them to help her know more about Jesus.

That is what it looks like to not compromise. That is what it looks like to put Jesus first. What we see in this story is that God showed up. Not everyone may have seen it, but God did show up. He showed up for the woman who died, and He gave her a peace that surpasses understanding. Then He rescued her soul and wiped away every tear as He took her up to heaven to dwell with Him forever. He greeted her after she died, and over the noise of the angels rejoicing, He may have said, "Listen, they are rejoicing over your sister. Because of your obedience, she now knows Me, too."

That is what our God is calling us to. He is calling us to stop acting like Esther. He is calling us to:

- stop concealing our faith because we are afraid we might lose a friendship.
- stop embracing the values of our culture over the values of Jesus.
- stop relying upon our money or friends or family or looks or intellect to help us make it through life.

Instead, He is calling us to live in utter dependence upon Him and upon His promises so that we can say with Paul that if Jesus isn't real and if He didn't rise again from the dead, then we ought to be pitied above all people (I Corinthians 15:19).

That is what God is calling each of us to, and the book of Esther comes to tell us that regardless of how we may have compromised in the past, there is hope for us. This book is named Esther because—despite her compromise—God didn't give up on her. Instead, He pursued her and saved her and changed her and used her to deliver His people.

That's the story you will find repeated over and over in the Bible. God takes sinners, compromisers, and failures, and He loves them and rescues them and then—bit by bit—He changes them and uses them for His glory.

That is the story of Abraham who lied to protect his wife; of Moses who once murdered an Egyptian; of David who slept with another man's wife; of Peter who denied Jesus again and again. This is the story of Paul, who persecuted the church—and if you will put your trust in Jesus, this can be your story.

Don't be shocked that Esther was not as good a person as you might have originally thought. The truth is that none of us are as good as we think we are.

But we serve a God Who is better than we ever thought He was, and He is able to do more for sinners than we could ever ask or imagine.

The reason He is able to do that is because He is a better savior than Esther was. All the heroes of the Bible compromised in one way or another—and because of that, none of them could ultimately offer us the salvation that you and I so desperately need.

But there is one Hero Who is different. Like Esther, this Hero grows up far away from home in a world full of temptation. Like Esther, this Hero is adopted by an earthly father. Like Esther, this Hero seems an unlikely candidate for royalty. And like Esther, this Hero is offered a kingdom if only He will compromise.

Matthew 4:8 says, "Again, the devil took him [Jesus] to a very high mountain and showed him all the kingdoms of the world and their glory. And he said to him, 'All these I will give you, if you will fall down and worship me.'"

On this mountain, that is all Jesus has to do. All the kingdoms of the world are set out before Him, and all He has to do is bow down and worship the devil. Jesus can have all the kingdoms of the world without an ounce of physical suffering. He can rule and reign as an earthly king over this entire world, and God won't even have to show up.

We serve a God Who is better than we ever thought He was. And He is able to do more for sinners than we could ever ask or imagine.

The thing is, Jesus knows what will happen if He says, "No." Jesus knows that if He turns down Satan's offer, it will mean suffering. In fact, Jesus knows that if He says, "No," to Satan, it will mean more suffering than any human being has ever endured in all of history.

Hear me. That day, on that mountain, Jesus is offered a choice:

a. more glory than any human being has ever had for compromising.

b. more suffering than any human being has ever experienced for putting God first.

These are Jesus' two options. Never in the history of the world has there been a greater temptation to compromise. But unlike Esther—and unlike you or me—Jesus says, "No." He says, "No," to everything that this world offers and chooses to follow God even though it brutally costs Him His life.

Jesus says to Satan, "Be gone, Satan! For it is written, 'You shall worship the LORD your God, and him only shall you serve'" (Matthew 4:10).

Jesus knows that no matter what it costs, only God is worthy of our worship. In the end, Jesus' choice leads Him to the cross. And there He endures all of the suffering that we deserve for our compromise. On the cross, the uncompromising Christ dies the compromiser's death.

Peter tells us that the way Jesus is able to endure it is because He entrusts Himself to His God (I Peter 2:23). On the cross, Jesus shows us what it looks like to live in utter dependence upon God. That is why the last thing Jesus says as he hangs upon the cross is, "Father, into your hands I commit my spirit" (Luke 23:46).

And then we wait to see what happens next. We wait to see if God will show up. Here is a man Who lived in utter dependence upon God, and so we wait to see if God will show up or not. For a little while, God seems conspicuously absent. For a little while as Jesus lies in that grave, everyone is confused and wonders where God is.

And then, at just the right moment, God shows up. On the third day, God raises Jesus from the dead, and gives Him a name above every name and an eternal kingdom that far exceeds anything that Satan had ever offered Him (Ephesians 1:21).

What we see in Jesus' life is that it is worth it. It is worth it to put God first. It is worth it to give up what you cannot keep to get what you can never lose. Jesus shows us what it looks like to live without compromise—and when we watch His life, we realize that as hard as it is, it is always worth it.

Not only is it worth it; but because Jesus died in our place, you and I can also be saved from all of our past compromise. Through His steadfast love, we can be changed bit by bit and used by God for His glory just like Esther was.

So let's be a people who repent of all our past compromises and look to Jesus for His forgiveness. And then, overwhelmed with His steadfast love, let us be a people who choose to follow Him no matter what. I promise you, it will be worth it.

CHAPTER 3: BEAUTY

Text: Esther 2

Now when the turn came for each young woman
to go in to King Ahasuerus . . . she was given
whatever she desired to take with her from the
harem to the king's palace.

Now Esther was winning favor in the eyes of all
who saw her. And when Esther was taken to King
Ahasuerus, into his royal palace . . . the king
loved Esther more than all the women, and she
won grace and favor in his sight more than all
the virgins, so that he set the royal crown on her
head and made her queen instead of Vashti.

(Esther 2:13-14, 15b-17)

WE LIVE IN a culture obsessed with physical beauty.
All you have to do is flip through the channels on
your TV or glance at the magazines at the check-out
stand or consider who the most popular actors and actresses are,
and you will realize how obsessed our culture is with physical
appearance. Think about the hours of TV that are spent discussing

what people wore to the Oscars and who was the best- and worst-dressed.

Never before has a culture been as barraged with images and information as we are today, and the vast majority of those images portray what our culture considers to be attractive people. You can't watch a movie or a TV show or a commercial without being confronted by images of the ideal body. One article states, "The media is littered with images of females who fulfill . . . unrealistic standards, making it seem as if it is normal for women to live up to this ideal."[3]

First-world media projects this standard of beauty that women are expected to aspire to, all the while knowing that the vast majority of women will never be able to achieve it. One author writes,

> Women almost always fall short of standards that are expected of them regarding physical appearance. Particularly for women, it is difficult to go through a day without viewing images that send the message, "you're not good enough." The pervasiveness of the media makes it very challenging for most women to avoid evaluating themselves against the sociocultural standard of beauty.[4]

---

[3] Kasey L. Serdar, "Female Body Image And The Mass Media: Perspectives On How Women Internalize The Ideal Beauty Standard," www.westminstercollege.edu/myriad, (unknown date).

[4] Melissa A. Milkie, "Social comparisons, reflected appraisals, and mass media: The impact of pervasive beauty images on Black and White girls' self-concepts," *Social Psychology Quarterly* 62, No. 2 (June 1999): 190-210.

The negative effects of this on women are astounding; but of course if you are a woman, you already know that. One author writes,

> The Psychological effects of the pursuit of the perfect female body include unhappiness, confusion, misery and insecurity. Women often believe that if only they had perfect looks, their lives would be perfectly happy; they blame their unhappiness on their bodies.[5]

The same author writes, "Obsessive concern about body shape and weight have become so common among American women of all ages that they now constitute the new norm."[6]

My heart breaks to think about the pain and tears and insecurities that many of you have experienced throughout your lives because people have chosen to judge you based on your physical appearance.

And of course women aren't the only ones who know the pain of being judged by the way they look. Most of us men have experienced insecurities based on our physical appearance as well. I remember years of my life where I wore hats and wondered if I would ever find a girlfriend who could look past the fact that I was going bald.

---

[5] Elayne A. Saltzberg and Joan C. Chrisler, "Beauty Is the Beast: Psychological Effects of the Pursuit of the Perfect Female Body," in *Women: A Feminist Perspective* (Mountain View, CA: Mayfield Publishing Company, 1995), 306-315.

[6] Ibid.

One day, I realized why I was so worried about people judging me based on my appearance: it was because that is precisely the way I was judging them.

Men, we don't judge women by their appearance simply because the media barrages us day in and day out with so many images of beautiful women. The media barrages us every day with images of beautiful women because they know that is exactly what we are looking for.[7]

And women, you don't spend your time and money and energy trying to look a certain way because that's what people look like on TV; you want to look a certain way because you believe that's what the real people in your life will find attractive. You want to look a certain way because you want to gain the acceptance and approval of others, and you know that the best way to get these things is through your appearance. You want to be somebody, and it seems like in order to be somebody, you need to be physically beautiful.

But is it really true that in order to be somebody, we need to live up to our culture's definition of beauty?

Are we really supposed to judge one another by our physical appearance? Single men and women, are you really supposed to decide who you will or won't date based solely on the way a person looks? Is our happiness really supposed to be determined by a number on a scale or a good/bad hair day or the clearness of our

---

[7] There is widespread debate over whether the media is prescriptive or descriptive. In other words, how much of our idea of beauty is driven by the media, and how much is the media simply giving us what we are looking for? My point is that we can't blame the media for our obsession with judging beauty by appearance. The media may influence what we think is beautiful, but the media is not what makes us judge others by appearance.

skin? We all know what our culture has told us about the importance of our physical appearance, but is our culture right?

To answer that last question, I want to go to the book of Esther where we quickly realize that the Persian culture is a lot like our own. The first person we meet in the book of Esther is King Ahasuerus who we soon find out is obsessed with external beauty. His couches are made of gold and silver; the pillars of his palace are made of marble; each of his drinking glasses is uniquely designed and covered with gold. Even the floors of his palace are made with a mosaic of pearls and marble and precious stones.

In Esther 1:11, we see that the king's obsession with beauty even includes his wife.

But the queen refuses to be treated like an object and paraded around before the people. She is a person, and people are far deeper than the way they look on the outside. Vashti demonstrates that by refusing to follow the king's request.

Now when the king hears this, he is furious and decrees that Vashti is never to see his face again, and, "her royal position [is to be given] to another who is better than she" (Esther 1:19).

The next chapter begins, "After these things, when the anger of King Ahasuerus had abated, he remembered Vashti and what she had done and what had been decreed against her" (Esther 2:1).

Alone without his queen, the king doesn't reevaluate if it was a good idea to send her away; instead, he blames her and the decree. The king's young men see that he isn't doing very well, and they come to the king and tell him that what he really needs to do is to replace Vashti. Right now, he might feel lonely, they say; but if he replaces Vashti, everything will be fine.

So we watch to see what it is going to take to replace Vashti. What are the important qualities of a wife that would please King Ahasuerus? What are the Persian people hoping to have in their queen?

In Esther 2:3, we see that the king and his officers believe that the only things necessary to make a good wife and queen are that she be beautiful, young, and a virgin. You know how some single people have a list of what they are looking for in a mate? The king also has a list.

So the king sends his officers into his entire kingdom to gather all the young beautiful virgins. Some commentators believe they may have gathered close to 1,000 women to undergo a year of beauty treatments.

One of the things that this passage does is show us what happens when a culture chooses to judge people based on their appearance. When we judge people by the external things of this world:

1. *People become replaceable.* Because all that the king looked for in a wife was external beauty, he found it very easy to discard one wife in order to take another. And we wonder why we have so many divorces and affairs, and why so many spouses struggle so deeply with insecurity.

2. *You can never be certain without trying them all.* Because he is the king, Ahasuerus doesn't just want a young and beautiful wife—he really wants to make sure he has the most beautiful woman possible. In order to be sure about that, he decides he needs to gather all the young beautiful virgins he can find and bring them all to the palace to try

them out. Is it any wonder why people are afraid to settle down and make commitments? They are always wondering if there might be someone better.

3. *No matter what you do, it will never be enough.* It isn't enough to be among the most beautiful women in the entire empire. To be good enough to spend a night with the king, these women have to go through a one-year beautifying treatment.

Now after one full year of preparation, each woman is ready to spend her one night with the king. She goes in to the king's room in the evening and leaves in the morning; but this time, she goes into another harem under the custody of another eunuch. Verse 14 says, "She would not go in to the king again, unless the king delighted in her and she was summoned by name."

These women were not allowed to go back to their families; they weren't allowed to get married. Most of the hundreds of women that were gathered would spend one night with the king and then for the rest of their lives would sit in luxurious isolation and dream about what might have been. No kids, no husband, no love, no family, no freedom—just their own wing of the palace to share with hundreds of other women just like them who aren't quite good enough.

This is the life that the empire offered: do everything you can to make yourself look beautiful and then maybe—if you are really good and do everything right—*maybe* the king will remember your name and call you again someday.

Beauty

When we read this chapter, we are blown away by how obsessed the king is with beauty and how easy it is for him to dispose of those who don't quite meet his standards.

Imagine the insecurities these women must feel. Surrounded by the most beautiful women in the empire, they are always looking over their shoulder, always comparing themselves to others, always obsessed with their flaws and how they don't think they are as pretty as the other women.

Even though Esther wins, Esther knows just how precarious her position as queen is. She knows that just down the hall are hundreds of the most beautiful women in the empire waiting to replace her if she slips up for even a moment. She knows that the only reason she is queen is because Vashti slipped up. She knows that her husband will have no qualms about getting rid of her either if she doesn't live up to his ridiculous standards. On the nights that he doesn't call her, she knows that he must be summoning one of the other women by name.

APPLICATION

The world of King Ahasuerus, where people were judged based on their appearance, was an absolute mess, wasn't it? And yet the reality is that we too live in a world obsessed with youth and beauty. It's a world that holds out an unrealistic standard of beauty and then expects women to go through beautifying treatments all their life in order to try to meet it. And it's never enough. Even if you succeeded yesterday at being beautiful, you still have to wake up today and start all over. You have to reapply makeup and redo your hair, and each day you live, you grow older and older and find it harder and harder to maintain the level of beauty that you need if you are going to be accepted by our culture.

Have you bought into the lie of our culture? Have you been judging other people by their appearance? Have you been judging yourself based on your appearance? Have you let the mirror determine if you are beautiful or not? Do you find yourself feeling confident and secure when you think you look good, and insecure and sad when you feel fat or ugly or your clothes don't seem to fit right?

Have you thrown yourself into the beautification treatments that our culture offers, hoping that by them you will finally achieve the beauty you have always longed for? Do you go to the gym—less in order to be healthy and more in order to look good? Do you believe that the way to find the acceptance and approval that you crave is by losing or gaining weight? Do you think that if you looked better, you would be happier?

Please hear me: it won't work. It will never be enough. Look at all the beautiful women in this chapter who bought into the lies of their culture. Look at how miserable their lives must have been. This story comes to show you the emptiness of pursuing our culture's obsession with beauty.

But I want to tell you that there is another way to live. You see, even though King Ahasuerus accurately represents the way our culture judges people, he is not the only king, and you don't have to marry him. You don't have to give yourself over to our culture's obsession with physical appearance, because you don't have to marry King Ahasuerus.

The Bible tells us about another King—Jesus—who comes to offer you His hand in marriage. But this King is different. This

King doesn't send His officers to find the healthiest and most attractive people in the world in order for Him to marry; instead this King gets off His throne and goes looking for His bride Himself. When He comes, He isn't looking for the healthy or for the beautiful or for the righteous; He comes looking for the sick and the spiritually ugly and the unrighteous, because this King comes to save sinners. He comes looking for the broken and needy whose lives lay in shambles so that He might rescue them with His love.

Romans 5:6-8 says it like this:

> For while we were still weak, at the right time Christ died for the ungodly. For one will scarcely die for a righteous person—though perhaps for a good person one would dare even to die—but God shows his love for us in that while we were still sinners, Christ died for us.

Not only is Jesus nothing like King Ahasuerus, Jesus is nothing like anyone else you have ever met in your entire life. Unlike everyone else, Jesus doesn't just love people who deserve it. This verse tells us that Jesus loved us while we were still weak, while we were stuck in our sins and addictions and failures—long before we ever loved Him. And unlike King Ahasuerus, Jesus doesn't wait for us to clean ourselves up before He lets us into His presence. Jesus came and shed His blood on the cross so that He might wash us white as snow. All of our sins, all of our failures, all of our shame and guilt—Jesus sees it all and has shed His blood to wash it all away.

Ephesians 5:25 tells us the kind of husband that Jesus came to be for His people. It says,

> Husbands, love your wives as Christ loved the church and gave himself up for her, that he might sanctify her, having cleansed her by the washing of water with the word, so that he might present the church to himself in splendor, without spot or wrinkle or any such thing, that she might be holy and without blemish.

Jesus calls the church His bride, and He died to wash us so that He might present us to Himself in splendor, without spot or wrinkle or any such thing. The beauty He offers penetrates to the very core of who we are, and it will never fade away. Because, you see, it is Jesus' love that makes us beautiful, and the Bible tells us that nothing in all the universe will ever separate God's people from His love.

I want you to know something: there is a reason that Jesus calls the church His bride. Have you ever been to a wedding and watched a groom as he stands there waiting to see his bride? Have you seen how intently he stares down the aisle as he waits for the doors to open? The smile on his face when he catches the first glimpse of his beautiful bride standing in all the splendor of her wedding dress—it's special, isn't it?

I will never forget watching the closed doors at my own wedding. I was staring so intently, I didn't even want to blink because I was afraid I would miss the first glimpse of Abbey as she came through the door. And when she did, she was absolutely beautiful. If you ask her, she will tell you she didn't like her hair;

but that's crazy, because I was there, and I saw her, and to this day, I still remember how beautiful she looked.

That is how Jesus sees the church. I know you don't always see yourself that way. I know others don't always see you that way. But Jesus does. If you have put your faith in Jesus, He has washed your sins away, and He has covered you with His glorious righteousness—and when He sees you, He sees you, "in splendor, without spot or wrinkle or any such thing" (Ephesians 5:25). That is your king. That is your husband. His love has made you beautiful.

That is your king. That is your husband.
His love has made you beautiful.

So take His love. Stop listening to the mirror, stop consulting the scale, stop trying to live up to a standard you will never be able to keep. Let your Savior's love make you beautiful. Unlike Ahasuerus, Jesus stands ready to welcome you just as you are. He has loved you and shed His blood on the cross so that He might make you truly beautiful. So take His love and find the joy and freedom that only it can bring.

Men, the truth is that we need this message as much as any woman does. Yes, we might not spend as many hours in front of a mirror, but we, too, care desperately what other people think about us. We, too, have bought into the lies of our culture that we need to be a certain way in order to be accepted. We have allowed the world's definition of beauty and success to define us.

And right now, we need to lay it all down and find our rest in the unfailing love of Jesus.

Now I want to end this chapter with one more specific application for all those who have a tendency to judge others by their appearances. (Men, this temptation is especially real for us.)

You see, while Jesus may be nothing like King Ahasuerus, the truth is that many of us have been. Honestly, how many of you have decided who you were attracted to based on their physical appearance? How many of you have ever chosen to date someone of questionable character because they were physically attractive? How many of you have passed up someone of exceptional character because they didn't meet your standard of beauty?

You may think that the king was a monster for sleeping with a different woman every night and then disregarding her without even remembering her name; but how many of you have ever brought an anonymous person into your room—on your computer or your phone—and used him or her for your own pleasure?

Our culture has lied to us about where true beauty is found, and we have believed the lie. Jesus came into a world that was consumed with physical beauty, and He was despised and rejected. Isaiah 53:2 tells us that Jesus, "had no form or majesty that we should look at Him, and no beauty that we should desire Him."

Please let this sink in. The Son of God was despised and rejected because people thought it was a good idea to judge each other by their appearance. The creator of the universe became a man and dwelt in human form, but the world missed Him because

Beauty

they were committed to judging people by their appearance. The devastating truth is that nothing has changed.

As long as people continue to judge based on appearances, they will continue to miss Jesus.

Hear this: You can't judge people by their appearances and Jesus by some other standard. You can only have one standard of beauty, and it must apply across the board.

So which one will it be? Will your standard of beauty be the shape of someone's body or a pretty face or flattering clothes? Is that how you will determine if you are attracted to someone or not?

If it is, you will never be attracted to Jesus. He hung naked on a bloody cross in shame and disgrace. But if you could only get beyond appearances and make a right judgment, then you would find that in all the universe, there has never been a more beautiful sight. There on that cross, the Son of God took our place. There, He bore our sin and gave us His righteousness. There, He poured out His love for His people so that whosoever would believe in Him might not perish but have everlasting life (John 3:16).

That is what true beauty looks like. When the poet George Herbert thought about Jesus hanging on the cross, he said, "Thou art my loveliness, my life, my light, beauty alone to me."[8]

Can you say that? Have you looked upon the cross and realized that Jesus truly is your loveliness, your life, your light, and beauty alone to you? I'm pleading with you. Will you let Jesus be beauty alone to you?

---

[8] George Herbert, "Dullness" in *The Works of George Herbert* (Wordsworth, 1994), 108.

Men, will you stop thinking you need a beautiful woman by your side to make you happy? Will you stop judging women by their appearances and make a right judgment? Women, will you let Jesus be beauty alone to you? Will you stop judging yourself based on your appearance? Will you stop dieting and going to the gym in search of beauty, and let Jesus' love cover you with all the beauty you need?

I promise you that if you will do this—if you will let Jesus be beauty alone to you, He will make you truly beautiful.

He will make you truly beautiful because He will cover you with Himself. One of Paul's favorite phrases is "In Christ." To be a Christian is to be "In Christ." And when you find that Jesus alone is beautiful, you will soon realize that because you are "In Christ," you too have been made beautiful.

So right now, please stop believing the lies that this world tells you about beauty. Say with me to Jesus, "You are my loveliness. Jesus, you are my life. You are beauty alone to me."

CHAPTER 4: CLIFFHANGER

Text: Esther 2:19-3:15

Letters were sent by couriers to all the king's provinces with instruction to destroy, to kill, and to annihilate all Jews, young and old, women and children, in one day, the thirteenth day of the twelfth month, which is the month of Adar, and to plunder their goods. A copy of the document was to be issued as a decree in every province by proclamation to all the peoples to be ready for that day. The couriers went out hurriedly by order of the king, and the decree was issued in Susa, the citadel. And the king and Haman sat down to drink, but the city of Susa was thrown into confusion.

(Esther 3:13-15)

WHEN ABBEY AND I were first married, someone loaned us Season One of the TV show *24* with lead character Jack Bauer. We were almost immediately hooked. The story had a hero that you could root for, and it had enemies that were so evil they defied imagination; of course, there were traitors working from the inside, and there were often incompetent leaders who didn't know that their job was simply to let Jack Bauer do whatever he thought was best.

I finally had to stop watching 24 because, instead of resolving, the end of each episode would actually escalate the situation. And the next day when I was trying to work, I often found that my mind would be distracted by trying to figure out what Jack Bauer was going to do next.

Well, this week I felt like I had gotten sucked back in, because the book of Esther reads a lot like an episode of 24. This "episode" begins innocently enough at a feast that the king is throwing in order to honor his new bride Esther. What the king doesn't know is that the woman he has chosen to be his queen is actually a Jewish orphan who has been raised right there in the capital, by a man who (most scholars believe) actually works for the king. His name is Mordecai.

After the feast is over, Mordecai is sitting at the king's gate when it comes to his attention that two of the king's servants (whose job is to guard the entrance to the king's private residence) are planning to assassinate the king. Mordecai immediately tells Esther, who in turn tells the king about the plan, making sure that the king knows that Mordecai is the one who discovered the plot, so that Mordecai can get the reward he deserves.

As soon as the king hears about it, he launches a full investigation—and sure enough, these two men are planning to kill him. So the king has the culprits hung on gallows, and then he has the entire episode about Mordecai's saving his life written down in a book.

Typically, the Persian kings were very good at rewarding people who proved themselves loyal to the king. So we wait to see what the king is going to do for Mordecai.

Chapter 3 begins, "After these things King Ahasuerus promoted . . ." and of course we expect to hear Mordecai's name. But instead, without giving us any explanation, the text says, ". . . promoted Haman the Agagite, the son of Hammedatha, and advanced him and set his throne above all the officials who were with him."

Any Jew who would have read this would have immediately seen the irony. Not only does Mordecai get passed up, but the king promotes Haman the Agagite. That is significant because the Agagites are descendants of the Amalekites, who are ancient tribal enemies of the Jews. There is a lot more that we could say here, but the main point is that Mordecai who deserves a promotion is passed up, and Haman whose people have always been enemies of the Jews is promoted instead.[9]

Not only is he promoted, but the king makes a law that says everyone has to bow down and pay homage to Haman when he passes by. This is simply too much for Mordecai. It seems like he reaches his limit and decides that this is where he will draw the line. So even though all the rest of the king's servants choose to bow down to Haman, Mordecai refuses.

Now the tension in the story begins to rise.

We watch as Haman passes by, and Mordecai refuses to bow. What's going to happen? How will Haman respond? What kind

---

[9] See Numbers 24:7 and I Samuel chapter 15. See also the Appendix of this book for more commentary on Haman's ancestral ties to the Jews.

of trouble will Mordecai get himself into? But Haman *doesn't notice*. For a moment, it seems like everything is going to be okay.

However, the king's servants do notice, and they go to Mordecai to find out what he could possibly be thinking. The Bible says day after day they talk to him—we assume, to try to convince him not to rock the boat and to just do what the king said—but Mordecai won't listen. Finally he tells them that the reason he won't bow down to Haman is because he is a Jew.

It's interesting to see where Mordecai chooses to draw the line. Because he is a Jew, Mordecai should have:

- returned to Jerusalem when Cyrus allowed the Jews to go home; but he hasn't.
- gone to Jerusalem to celebrate the feast; but we see that it's a few days before the Passover, and here he is in Susa.
- encouraged Esther, who always obeys him, to be like Daniel and not defile herself with the king's food; instead, he has told her to conceal her faith.

However, when it comes to bowing down before Haman the Agagite, this is where Mordecai draws the line.

So when the king's servants realize that they are not going to convince Mordecai to bow down to Haman, they decide to talk to Haman and see if Mordecai can get a free pass because he is Jewish.

The tension is back. I have a sneaking suspicion that Mordecai's being Jewish isn't going to fly as an excuse.

After Haman receives the oh-so-shocking news that someone dares not to bow down to him, he decides he needs to see this for himself. You can hear the music beginning to play in the background as Haman gets ready to go outside and see if it's really true.

Haman makes his way to the city gates. He watches as everyone he passes bows down before him. And then he sees Mordecai in the distance. He watches as he gets closer; tension is rising with every step.

Everyone standing around Mordecai falls to their knees, but there Mordecai stubbornly stands. Haman can feel the blood rushing to his face; his stomach knots up and moves into his chest, and he is, "filled with fury" (Esther 3:5). As you watch, you wonder if he might be angry enough to run into the crowd and strangle Mordecai with his own bare hands.

But he doesn't. Maybe he isn't as angry as we thought. Maybe we have been blowing this whole thing out of proportion. Or maybe he just doesn't want to get his own hands dirty. Maybe he is going to send someone else to get rid of Mordecai.

Fortunately, the Bible doesn't leave us guessing as to why Haman doesn't go after Mordecai himself. I love the way the NIV translates this because it makes Haman's motivation really clear. It says,

> When Haman saw that Mordecai would not kneel down or pay him honor, he was enraged. Yet having learned who Mordecai's people were, he scorned the idea of killing only Mordecai. Instead Haman looked for a way to destroy all Mordecai's people, the Jews, throughout the whole kingdom of Xerxes." (Esther 3:5-6, NIV)

Let that sink in. Because Mordecai disrespects him, Haman thinks every single Jewish person in the world should have to die. The reason he doesn't go into that crowd and strangle Mordecai for refusing to bow isn't because that would be too barbaric or over the top—it's because that would be way too small. His pride is so great that he scorns the idea that killing one person can make up for the fact that Mordecai doesn't respect him.

Let me put this in perspective. That would be like the president of a country riding in his limo down the street and seeing a man with a sign that says, "I don't like your foreign policy." All of the sudden, the president stops the car and calls for his agents. However, he doesn't tell them to simply take this man's sign away; he doesn't tell them to throw him in jail or beat him up or even kill him. Instead, he has his agents find out what ethnicity he is from. Then the president gets the military to round up every one who has the same ethnicity as this man and ships them all to Antarctica where he will deploy one of his nuclear bombs on them.

That sounds over the top, maybe a little crazy; but that is what we see happening in this story. That is the way Haman thinks, and Haman happens to be the second-most powerful man in the world. Now you start to see why this is shaping up to be an episode of 24.

Now that you know just how crazy this guy is, you start to watch him very carefully. What you see is that he goes home and gets a calendar, and his servants grab some dice. He watches as they pick a day and roll the dice and then cross out the day. And then they pick the next day and throw the dice and cross it out. You watch until you are almost tired of watching. Then all of the sudden, the dice rolls what he is looking for, cheers go up, and a day is circled on the calendar. That will be the day that Haman will seek to wipe out all of the Jews from the face of the earth. The camera zooms in so that you can see the day the dice chose: 11 months from now.

Having chosen the day, Haman heads immediately to the palace to see the king. You can tell by his face that he has a plan. When he gets to the king he says to him,

> "There is a certain people scattered abroad and dispersed among the peoples in all the provinces of your kingdom. Their laws are different from those of every other people, and they do not keep the king's laws, so that it is not to the king's profit to tolerate them. If it please the king, let it be decreed that they be destroyed, and I will pay 10,000 talents of silver into the hands of those who have charge of the king's business, that they may put it into the king's treasuries." (Esther 3:8b-9)

Haman's plan is unveiled. He wants to use the king to make one of those decrees that can never be revoked, in order to kill all of the Jews. But notice his cunning:

- Haman doesn't even tell the king who the people are. He keeps them impersonal—the only description he gives the king is that they don't keep his laws. No proof, just Haman's word.
- Haman goes on to tell the king that it doesn't profit him to keep these people around; but of course, he gives no

evidence for this claim either. In actuality, the evidence is quite the opposite, because without the Jews, the king would not be married to Esther. In fact, without the Jews, the king would be dead, because Mordecai had saved his life.

- Before the king can ask him for more details, Haman offers him what he knows the king really cares about: money. Haman shows the king that it would be profitable for him to destroy these people because he will give the king 10,000 talents of silver.[10]

Now at this point if you were the king, you might be thinking, "It would probably be a good idea for me to ask a few questions. Maybe I should get a little bit more information before ordering the slaughter of an entire people group." Maybe you would want to know who exactly these people were. Maybe you might want at least one example of how they had hurt your empire. Maybe you would want to know why Haman had such a grudge against these people or even where he thought he was going to get all the money he promised. Haman's argument leaves you with a lot of questions, doesn't it?

But this king doesn't ask any questions at all. He doesn't care. All he cares about is himself, and Haman just gave him 10,000 reasons to destroy this people—whoever they happen to be. So the Bible tells us that the king, "took his signet ring from his hand

---

[10] Ian M. Duguid, *Esther and Ruth* (Phillipsburg: P&R Publishing, 2005), 39. That was a ridiculously large amount of money – well over half of the empire's annual tax revenue.

and gave it to Haman the Agagite . . . the enemy of the Jews" (Esther 3:10). He tells him to do whatever seems good to him.

So Haman takes the ring and writes a law in the name of the king, and he seals it with his ring. The law instructs the people, "to destroy, to kill and to annihilate all Jews, young and old, women and children, in one day . . . and to plunder all of their goods" (Esther 3:13). Haman sends out an order to wipe all of God's people off of the face of the earth—and with them, all of God's promises of salvation.

The order is translated into all the different languages and carried to the farthest reaches of the empire. Then Haman and the king sit down for a drink while, "the city of Susa [is] thrown into confusion" (Esther 3:15b).

Can you imagine what it must have been like to live in that empire? To know that if one person from your race were to show disrespect to someone, it might end up costing you and your entire family their lives? To know that all that the people in power cared about was money, and that they would commit genocide for the right price?

We get depressed and think the world is going to end when the guy we want to be president doesn't win. We are up in arms when any of our rights seems to be threatened. Can you imagine what it must have been like to know that your life lay in the hands of men like Haman and King Ahasuerus? These men have no qualms about ordering genocide and then sitting down and enjoying a drink together.

So, after writing the order and sending it throughout the empire, Haman sits down thinking that his plan has been accomplished. But he is forgetting something. You know in the movies, after the bad guys think that the hero has been killed, they finally relax and sit back to celebrate, confident that now there is nothing that can stop them? That is what is happening here.

But you know what happens in the movies, right? The hero everyone thinks is dead suddenly rises from the rubble. In this story, we will soon see that the Hero that Haman and the king have overlooked isn't dead. Now He might be hidden, and He certainly hasn't shown His face the way His people expected Him to; but He isn't dead. Soon we will see that Haman has been a fool to forget about Him.

Haman may have thought that the stars were in control of the dice, and that his gods were picking the best possible day for the massacre. But he was wrong. Proverbs 16:33 says, "The lot is cast into the lap, but its every decision is from the LORD." You see, it was the Lord Who caused the lots to fall far enough away that He would have 11 months to orchestrate His rescue plan.

And you remember when the king said to Haman, ". . . the people also [are given to you], to do with them as it seems good to you" (Esther 3:11b)? Well, the people weren't the king's to give away; they were God's people, and God would not be bribed so easily.

APPLICATION

In this chapter, you won't get to see exactly how this Hero will save His people, but what you need to know is that He is alive, that He has a plan, and that He will succeed.

That is one of the messages that the book of Esther teaches us: God is in control even when we don't see Him. From the moment Haman has come on the scene, this story has gone from bad to worse until it seems like all of God's people will be killed and all of His promises made void.

But that isn't what happens in this story, because even when you can't see Him, God is in control. The Hero is alive, He has a plan, and He will save His people.

I don't know what you are going through right now. I don't know what's overwhelming you today. I don't know what part of your life you are struggling to see God in or to understand what He is doing. But what I do know is this:

- Your God is alive.
- He has a plan.
- If you will trust Him, He will save you.

Period.

Another thing we realize in this story is that we are far more like King Ahasuerus than we would like to admit. Now when we read this story, it's pretty easy to look down on Ahasuerus, isn't it? I mean how blind must he have been to let Haman play him with his shallow logic? How selfish can you be to be willing to kill off an entire race of people for money? Why would you ever give someone as evil as Haman your signet ring and let him control you like that? It's easy to think, "If I were king, I would rule with justice. If I were king, I would only listen to people I knew I could trust. If I were king, I would never give up control to someone who might misuse it."

We need to be careful, though, because this story is far more like our own story than we would like to admit. The Bible tells us that you and I have an enemy far more conniving than Haman, and that he is daily seeking after the signet ring of our lives. Our enemy comes after us just like Haman went after the king—by appealing to our selfishness with his shallow logic and empty promises.

The enemy comes to tell you that God doesn't really care about you and that you can't trust His promises. He comes to tell you that following God will be hard, and not worth it. He comes to tell you that if you will just give him the signet ring of your life, he will satisfy your longings and fill your treasury with good things.

Haven't you ever heard his logic before? Haven't you heard him say things like:

- Trusting God will never take away your loneliness—but if you found the right boy or the right girl, then you would truly be happy.
- Following Jesus is not nearly as satisfying as giving into your lust—but if you give in, so you will get the feelings of satisfaction you are longing for.
- God's attention and approval aren't enough—but if you exaggerate a little bit, or if you lie a little bit, or if you flirt a little bit, then you will get the attention and approval that you crave.

How many times have we heard this kind of shallow logic and (like the king) given in without so much as a question? How many times have we traded our integrity for a laugh or our purity for a moment of passing pleasure?

You see, we don't ask questions, because we want to believe the enemy. We want to believe that there will be no consequences for our actions. Think about the king: he wants to think that he can give Haman his signet ring and take his 10,000 talents, and that there won't be any consequences for it. That is what he wants to believe, and Haman has purposely left out any of the consequences so that the king won't have to think about them. But just because he has left them out doesn't mean they aren't there.

There are consequences every time we give away the signet ring of our life. If Haman had his way, the king would lose his wife, and the man who saved the king's life would be hung publicly on a gallows. In fact, if Haman ultimately had his way, then all of the good promises of God for the Jews and for all of humanity would be wiped out, and we would all live in utter hopelessness. Those were the consequences of Haman's plot, though he didn't mention them or even know about some of them.

And the consequences haven't changed. To this day, the devil goes around like a roaring lion looking for someone to devour with his deceptive tongue (I Peter 5:8). He is our enemy, and he longs to steal from us everything good and lasting in our lives.

But he doesn't tell us that. No, he tells us that he wants to make us happy, that he wants to take our loneliness away, he wants to make us rich, or wants to bring us immediate satisfaction. He tells us that he is our friend.

I am begging you to stop being deceived. Stop believing him when he tells you that it's okay to follow your feelings. Stop following him when he promises you immediate gratification without any consequences. Just slow down. Please just slow down and investigate. If you do, this is what you will find.

You will find that the story of Esther is part of a bigger story about an even greater king. This King is the creator of the entire world—and ultimately, it is His empire that you and I find ourselves living in. This King is worthy of our worship, and He has given us good laws to follow so that we might live life to its fullness. But you and I have not followed His laws the way we should; because of that, this King has far more reason to act against us than Ahasuerus had to act against the Jews.

We have rebelled against this King; we have committed treason against this King; we have done everything we can to dethrone this King so that we can have control over our own lives. That is why this King has every reason to treat us like His enemies. Not only have we committed treason, but also we have an enemy far greater than Haman who loves to come before God and present to Him all the reasons why it would be in His best interest to destroy us.

The Bible calls our enemy the accuser because, like Haman, he loves to accuse us before our King. Do you understand what this means? It means that if God were anything like King Ahasuerus, He would send out a decree for our destruction and sit down to have a drink. In fact, if God were anything like you or me, He would hand over His signet ring knowing that it would not profit Him to keep us alive. But the book of Esther comes to tell us that our King isn't like Ahasuerus—and He isn't like us either.

That is why, when Satan stood before Him asking for the right to destroy His people like they deserved, God said, "No. No, you can't have My people." And for a moment Satan couldn't believe what he heard because it seemed like God wasn't being just. God's people deserved destruction; if God were going to be just, then He couldn't simply say, "No."

Here, we begin to see God's logic, which is deeper than anything we could ever ask or imagine. Here, God doesn't just tell Satan, "No." Instead, he takes His Son—His only Son, Whom He loves—and He says to Satan, "Here, take Him and do to Him what seems good to you, for my Son has willingly chosen to take the punishment that my people deserve." Where King Ahasuerus takes money to destroy an innocent people, God gives His only Son in order to save sinners.

Where King Ahasuerus takes money to destroy an innocent people, God gives His only Son in order to save sinners.

That is why in the Bible, it's not the Jews who are destroyed and killed and annihilated; rather, it is God's only Son Who is hung upon a cross while His few earthly goods are plundered by men who roll dice for His clothes. His body is destroyed. He is the One killed so that our King can let us go free.

Romans 3:23-25 explains God's glorious logic when it says,

> For all have sinned and fall short of the glory of God, and are justified by his grace as a gift, through the redemption that is in Christ Jesus, whom God put forward as a propitiation by his blood to be received by faith. This was

to show God's righteousness, because in his divine forbearance he had passed over former sins. It was to show his righteousness at the present time, so that he might be just and the justifier of the one who has faith in Jesus.

Listen to the logic of that text. All have sinned and fallen short of the glory of God and so deserve to experience the wages of their sin which is eternal death. But God says, "No!" because he wants to be the justifier of His people. He wants to be the One Who saves sinners.

Satan says, "That is not fair. You can't be both the just *and* the justifier—you have to pick one or the other. Either save Your people and no longer be just and worthy of worship; or give up being the justifier and let Your people be destroyed like they deserve."

But God says, "No! I *can* be just and the justifier, and I *will* be just and the justifier, even if it costs me everything." And so He puts forward His Son to bear our punishment on the cross in our place. (That is what the word propitiation is talking about.) He does it all so that He might save us.

In case you are starting to feel sorry for God's only Son, Jesus, you don't have to. God raised Him again from the dead and has given Him a seat at His right hand where He will rule and reign over the people He bought with His blood for all eternity.

That is your King. He comes to you right now to ask you for the signet ring of your life. He comes to you and says, "If you will give Me control; if you will submit to Me as your King; if you will let Me, I will save you, I will rescue you, and I will wash away your sins."

You don't have to live like Ahasuerus anymore. You don't have to believe the shallow logic that offers you temporary pleasure while hiding the eternal consequences. You don't have to let your feelings or people's opinions or the culture's whims control you anymore. You have a good King Who deserves your worship.

So won't you bow before Him now? He has stood up to your enemy and told him, "No!" And now He offers to hold your soul in the palm of His hand where no one can get to it (John 10:28-19). So won't you give your life to the One who gave His life for you?

CHAPTER 5: DEVASTATION

Text: Esther 4

Then Mordecai told . . . Esther, "Do not think to
yourself that in the king's palace you will escape
any more than all the other Jews. For if you keep
silent at this time, relief and deliverance will rise
for the Jews from another place, but you and your
father's house will perish. And who knows
whether you have not come to the kingdom for
such a time as this?"

(Esther 4:13-14)

MOST OF YOU have probably seen a movie about the
end of the world. Usually in this type of movie, there
is a meteorite that is headed toward earth, and it's
clear that there will be no survivors. The news anchor shares the
devastating news about how much time the world has left with
as much composure as he can muster; but, despite his call to stay
calm, the entire world is thrown into confusion. Some people just
stand there stunned by the news, some begin to loot and burn
and throw off all restraints, others run to drugs or alcohol or sex,
or frantically search for their loved ones.

Devastation

The movies that do a good job of telling this story invite you to contemplate how you would respond if you were ever faced with a similar situation.

What we see in this chapter of Esther is that the Jews have just heard the news report that their world is going to end in about 11 months.

Imagine you are summoned, along with everyone else, to the city gates to hear the latest decree from the king. The crowd goes silent as a man clears his throat and begins to read. You listen to what the man says, and you feel like it must be some kind of bad dream. This decree contains specific instructions for people to kill, destroy, and annihilate all Jews—young and old, women and children—on a specific day approximately 11 months from now. This order comes down from the king and cannot be revoked.

The story is inviting you in, asking you to consider how you would respond if something like this happened to you. This is an invitation that we can't afford to ignore because we all really do face a very similar decree. II Peter 3:10 says, "But the day of the Lord will come like a thief. And then the heavens will pass away with a roar, and the heavenly bodies will be burned up and dissolved, and the earth and the works that are done on it will be exposed."

I Thessalonians 5:2-3 says it like this:

> For you yourselves are fully aware that the day of the LORD will come like a thief in the night. While people are saying, "There is peace and security," then sudden destruction will come upon them as labor pains come upon a pregnant woman, and they will not escape.

The world is ending; the date has been set, all of our works will be exposed, and each of us will stand before our God to give an account of our lives. On that day, the heavens and the earth and everything we have worked for and clung to will be dissolved. The decree is real; the only question is, how will we respond to it?

When the Jews in Susa hear the tragic news, the entire city is thrown into confusion. Esther chapter 4 begins by telling us how Mordecai responds when he hears the news: "When Mordecai learned all that had been done, Mordecai tore his clothes, and put on sackcloth and ashes, and went out into the midst of the city, and he cried out with a loud and bitter cry" (Esther 4:1).

But Mordecai does more than just weep; he goes to the entrance of the king's gate, hoping to get word to Esther. He knows he has to try to fix the situation.

Esther hears that her adopted father is deeply distressed. She hears that he has torn his clothes and is at the palace gate lying in sackcloth and ashes. So do you know what she does? You might think she would ask him what is wrong or if there was anything she could do to help him. But no, Esther sends him a new set of clothes.

In verse 3, we read that all of the Jews in the entire empire have found out about this decree and are weeping, but Esther has no idea what is going on. Notice what life in the palace has done to her; it has isolated her from God's people and made her callous to their needs. Esther has forgotten who she is and where she came from. Esther has so embraced the pagan culture of the palace that she doesn't even want to know what is causing her adoptive

father to weep. She just wants to pretend that everything is okay.
So she sends Mordecai a new set of clothes, hoping they will help
him pretend as well.

How many of us have chosen to live like Esther? How many
of us are living as if the day of the LORD isn't coming—living as
if this world is all there is, as if we are going to get to keep all of
the things we are working so hard to accumulate, as if the most
important thing in the world is our present happiness?

Many of us have never felt like Mordecai feels in this passage.
Many of us have never felt the crushing weight of the impending
destruction that the Bible says each of us deserves. Instead, we
are living like Esther.

I am not saying that we don't believe in our heads that heaven
or hell exists; what I am saying is that we have not let the infinite
weight of their existence impact our lives. We give more thought
and attention to what we are going to eat today or who we are
going to hang out with than we do to where we are going to spend
eternity.

Tell me that isn't true. Tell me that today, you have not
thought more about what you were going to eat or what you were
going to wear to work or what you were going to do after work or
what you had planned for the weekend, than you did to where
you would spend eternity and why you would spend it there.

II Peter 3:11-12a makes it clear that the coming day of the
LORD ought to affect the way we live: "Since all these things are
thus to be dissolved, what sort of people ought you to be in lives
of holiness and godliness, waiting for and hastening the coming
of the day of God . . . "

So the coming day of the LORD ought to affect our lives, but how? In order to help us answer that question, I want to take a look at how Mordecai responds to the king's decree.

The first thing we see is that he refuses the clothes that Esther sends. So Esther sends her servant to find out what the problem is. In verse 7, Mordecai tells him all that has happened, including the exact sum of money that Haman has promised to pay into the king's treasuries for the destruction of the Jews. Mordecai also gives the servant a copy of the written decree issued in Susa for their destruction, to show it to Esther. He tells the servant to explain the decree to her and, "command her to go to the king to beg his favor and plead with him on behalf of her people"(Esther 4:8b).

Remember in Esther 2:20, we saw that, "Esther obeyed Mordecai just as when she was brought up by him." So Mordecai assumes that he is in control and will be able to get Esther to do what he asks and, "go to the king and beg his favor and plead with him on behalf of her people."

Notice the language Mordecai uses here. Normally in the Bible when we read this kind of language, it's describing people talking to God. Normally when the Jews would fast and put on sackcloth, they would go to God and beg Him for mercy and plead with Him; but that is not what Mordecai is doing here. Mordecai still thinks he can get the Jews out of this situation on his own, and at least for now is trusting in politics to save them.

Do you see how easy it is for us to respond like Mordecai? Like Mordecai, many of us want to be fixers. We hear about a problem, and our first thought goes to how we might fix it. This is a temptation that I am constantly facing in my own life. I don't know how many times my wife has come to me with a problem, and I have listened and tried to show her empathy even though the whole time I am wanting to blurt out the answer to the problem. I wait and nod and, after I feel like I have listened long enough and shown enough empathy, I tell her how she can fix the problem. Then she will say something like, "I really don't need you to try to fix the problem. What I was hoping was that you would pray with me about it."

That's when I realize how stupid I have been. What my wife is really saying is that she knows that this problem is bigger than me and that even my best ideas won't fix it. My wife realizes that what she really needs is God; what she really wants from me isn't advice but acknowledgment that we need God.

It is time that we admit that you and I can't fix the things that matter most, and we certainly can't get ourselves ready for the coming day of the LORD.

Malachi 3:1-2 says,

> Behold, I send my messenger, and he will prepare the way before me. And the LORD whom you seek will suddenly come to his temple; and the messenger of the covenant in whom you delight, behold, he is coming, says the LORD of hosts. But who can endure the day of his coming, and who can stand when he appears?

The Jews in Malachi thought they were ready; they thought that they had prepared themselves for the coming of the LORD. That's why they were seeking it—because they thought they were better than everyone else, and that when God came, He would affirm them. But Malachi comes to tell them that they aren't ready; that when God comes, they will find that they can't stand before Him in their own strength.

You and I cannot stand before God in our own strength. We are not good enough to stand before Him. The weight of His glorious perfection will crush every sinner who tries to stand before Him on their own. Mordecai was a fool to think he could fix this problem on his own, and you and I are fools when we think that we can somehow stand before God in our own strength.

Listen to how Esther responds to Mordecai's command. She says in verse 11,

> "All the king's servants and the people of the king's provinces know that if any man or woman goes to the king inside the inner court without being called, there is but one law—to be put to death, except the one to whom the king holds out the golden scepter so that he may live. But as for me, I have not been called to come in to the king these thirty days."

It's kind of ironic that when Esther wasn't really in that much danger at all, Mordecai had told Esther to hide her identity in order to protect herself. And now when every single Jew in the world is sentenced to death, he wants her to expose her identity.

But it's not as easy as Mordecai thinks. Esther has taken his advice. She has compromised to fit in; she has embraced the empire and their values; she has become the woman Mordecai told her to become—and now she isn't going to go back just because he commands her to.

Basically, Esther is telling Mordecai, "It would be suicide to go before the king, and you know it." There is only one law for those who go before the king without being summoned: death, unless the king holds out his scepter. Esther finds that favor highly unlikely, because the king hasn't called for her in over 30 days—and everyone knows that the king never sleeps alone. For 30 days, Esther has been sleeping alone, knowing that her husband has been sleeping with another woman; so you can understand how she might doubt that her husband would be all that happy to see her.

So it sounds like this is it. It sounds like they are at an impasse. Esther was Mordecai's only chance, and now he learns that she isn't going to go into the king. Mordecai has come to the end of himself. He doesn't have a plan B. He realizes he isn't in control anymore.

Has that ever happened to you? Have you ever come to the place where you realize you aren't in control? Have you ever realized that you can't fix the things that you have broken? That is what Mordecai finally realizes here.

What we see is that Mordecai's need becomes the fertile soil for God to begin to work. For the first time in this book, someone gives up on themselves and chooses to trust God. Coming to the end of himself, Mordecai realizes that God is his only hope. Listen to what he says next—and I want you to notice how Mordecai's logic depends entirely on God showing up. He says to Esther,

> "Do not think to yourself that in the king's palace you will escape any more than all the other Jews. For if you keep silent at this time, relief and deliverance will rise for the

Jews from another place, but you and your father's house will perish. And who knows whether you have not come to the kingdom for such a time as this?" (Esther 4:13-14)

I want you to let this blow you away. You would expect Mordecai to respond to Esther's comments with more desperation than ever; instead, Mordecai is suddenly, strangely confident. Basically, he tells Esther that the Jews don't need her. If she doesn't come through, then deliverance will come from somewhere else. Notice that Mordecai is no longer casting all his hope on Esther; instead, he has placed his hope on God and God alone.

That explains why Mordecai is able to cling to his hope in deliverance without having any idea exactly how God will deliver His people. That is what faith looks like. Mordecai has no idea how God will save His people; but he refuses to believe that God will break His promise, so he is able to be at peace. Mordecai gives up control. Esther can do whatever she wants, and God will still take care of His people.

Mordecai is no longer casting all his hope on Esther; instead, he has placed his hope on God alone.

But how could Mordecai know for certain that God would keep His promises? How could he know that God would deliver His people? It's because when Mordecai looked back on Israel's history, he realized that no matter how impossible the situation, God always kept His promises:

- When Sarah was 90 years old, God kept His promise and gave her a son.
- When Sarah's son Isaac was on the altar and Abraham's knife was coming down toward him, God kept His promise and rescued him.
- When Abraham's descendants had become a nation, and all of Pharaoh's army was about to come down on Israel and destroy them, God parted the Red Sea and saved His people.

And now with Mordecai's back to the wall, with no plan B, with the Persian Empire seemingly aligned against him, Mordecai chooses to trust that God will keep His promises.

Notice that he urges Esther to do the same. Before, Mordecai has always feared the empire; but now, for the first time in the story, Mordecai begins to fear God.

Mordecai has woken up and realized that at the end of the day, it's God and not the empire Who will have the last word. And because of that, it's God Whom Mordecai now begs Esther to align herself with. Yet Mordecai does more than merely threaten her with God's power to judge; he also encourages her with God's power to change.

Mordecai sends word back to Esther and says, "Who knows whether you have come to the kingdom for such a time as this?" (Esther 4:14b). He wants Esther to know that God can use her, even after all she has done. Imagine how scared Esther must be. She knows it is a frightening thing to stand up to the king. She knows that her life will be in danger. For the last few years, she has taken all her comfort from her relationship with the king; now she is being asked to put it all on the line. You remember that she has given up her relationship with God in order to have a relationship with the king; now she is afraid that if she loses her relationship with the king, she won't have anything.

But Mordecai tells her that God isn't done with her. Even though she has given up on God, He hasn't abandoned her, He hasn't given up pursuing her, and—if she will trust Him—He is still able to use her.

When Esther hears this, she changes. When she realizes that the God she has abandoned has not abandoned her but is able to use her even after all she has done, she decides to trust Him. Even if it costs Esther her life, she decides she wants her God back. Esther realizes that life in the palace without God isn't worth it. In fact, Esther realizes that life itself without God isn't worth it.

So she says to Mordecai,

> "Go gather all the Jews to be found in Susa, and hold a fast on my behalf, and do not eat or drink for three days, night or day, and I and my young women will also fast as you do. Then I will go to the king, though it is against the law, and if I perish, I perish." (Esther 4:16)

Notice how Esther has chosen to throw herself on the mercy of God. She is about to go before the king, and she won't be able to say a word before he looks at her and decides to welcome her or to kill her. We have already seen how this king makes his decisions, haven't we? He judges everything by appearance.

Devastation

If Esther had chosen to go before the king in her own strength, then she might have had other people fast and pray. But she would have spent all her time finding the right outfit and getting a makeover and doing everything she could to please the king with her appearance. But she doesn't. Instead, she does the opposite. She chooses not to eat or drink for three days before seeing the king. That means she won't be looking her best. What she is saying is, "I am letting go of control, I am done doing things my way, I will no longer try to earn the king's favor through my looks." She is saying, "I am throwing myself upon the mercy of my God." If the king accepts her, it will be because God intervened. For the first time, Esther is living in such a way that if God doesn't show up, she will perish.

Well, God does show up. God shows up for Esther, and He shows up for the Jewish people. He delivers them out of the hands of Haman. Even when it seems impossible, God shows up. Even after everything they have done to ignore Him, God shows up and saves the Jews from the death that they have been sentenced to. He saves them by using Esther to be their mediator—by using Esther to go before the king and plead with him on their behalf.

APPLICATION

We have already seen that we are all born into just as dire a situation as the one the Jews faced. Actually, our situation is even worse because the King we have offended is far more powerful than King Ahasuerus. Our King doesn't merely control our physical lives; He holds our eternal destiny in His hand. Like Mordecai, you and I can't get access to this King. We can't get to

Him because sinners can neither dwell in His presence nor endure the crushing weight of God's glorious perfection.

Like Mordecai and the Jews, we need a mediator. We need someone with access to God who will plead with Him on our behalf. In order for this mediator to plead with God on our behalf, He is going to have to understand us. He is going to have to know something about what it's like to be human. But even more than that, for this mediator to truly plead with God on our behalf, He is going to have to find something good in us, something that would justify God's pardoning us.

Contrary to the world's opinion, the Bible makes it clear that it is not that easy to find something good in us. Isaiah 59:11b-13a talks about our situation when it says,

> We hope for justice, but there is none; for salvation, but it is far from us. For our transgressions are multiplied before you, and our sins testify against us; for our transgressions are with us, and we know our iniquities: transgressing, and denying the LORD, and turning back from following our God . . . .

That is our situation. We hope for salvation; but no matter how hard we try, we aren't good enough to earn it. We long to somehow earn God's love, but the reality is that even our best works are nothing but filthy rags.

Isaiah 59:15b-16a continues to describe our situation. It says, "The LORD saw it, and it displeased him that there was no justice. He saw that there was no man, and wondered that there was no one to intercede." We need a mediator, someone to intercede for us; but of all the people in this world, there isn't one person good enough to stand in God's presence.

But listen to how God responded to our situation. Instead of simply giving us the judgment that we deserve, it says, "Then his [God's] own arm brought him salvation, and his righteousness upheld him" (Isaiah 59:16b).

God sent Someone to intercede for us. This Mediator has complete access to God the Father because He is none other than Jesus Christ, the Son of God. And yet, this Mediator understands us, because the Son of God took on flesh and became human and dwelt among us. I Timothy 2:5 says, "There is one mediator between God and men, the man Christ Jesus."

But still we have the problem of what this Mediator is going to say to God in order to justify us. What will Jesus use to plead with God on our behalf?

The answer is His own righteousness. In order to save us, Jesus shed His blood on the cross to forgive us of our sins and to clothe us with His righteousness.

II Corinthians 5:21 says it like this: "For our sake he [God] made him [Jesus] to be sin who knew no sin, so that in him we might become the righteousness of God."

Our mediator took our place and died our death so that in Him we might become pleasing to God. On the cross, Jesus took our sin upon Himself so that in Him we might become the righteousness of God.

Please hear me. Jesus is our Mediator, and He is an even better mediator than Esther. Jesus didn't just *risk* His life to save us; He actually *gave* His life in order to save us. Jesus didn't say, "If I perish, I perish." He said, "Let Me perish so that they might live." That is the kind of Mediator we have.

This Mediator has done more than just save us from hell; He has actually opened up a way for us to have access to God. Jesus has washed us with His blood, and He has given us His righteousness so that now we can have access to the God of the universe anytime we want.

Hebrews 10:19-22 says,

> Therefore, brothers, since we have confidence to enter the holy places by the blood of Jesus, by the new and living way that He opened for us through the curtain, that is, through his flesh, and since we have a great priest over the house of God, let us draw near with a true heart in full assurance of faith, with our hearts sprinkled clean from an evil conscience and our bodies washed with pure water.

We live in a broken world full of many heartbreaking problems, but we don't have to face this world alone. We have been given access to the Creator of the universe through His only Son, Jesus. That means we don't have to ignore the brokenness of this world like Esther did, and we don't have to try to fix it in our own strength like Mordecai did.

Instead, you and I can take the brokenness of this world and go to our God and plead with Him for mercy. We can go to Him and beg Him for help, and we can know beyond a shadow of a doubt that the God, Who gave His only Son to be our Mediator, will deliver us. Even when you don't see where deliverance is

Devastation

coming from, even when you have no idea what God is doing, you can go before Him with full assurance that the God who gave His only Son on your behalf will rescue you.

We don't even have to fear the day of the LORD anymore. On the cross, Jesus bore the punishment of the day of the LORD in our place so that now we no longer have to fear His coming. In fact, for all those who have put their trust in Jesus and chosen to align themselves with God, the day of the LORD will be the beginning of an eternity of joy with Him. That is why His people can say with the Apostle John, "Amen. Come, Lord Jesus!" (Revelation 22:20).

CHAPTER 6: PROVIDENCE

Text: Esther 5-6

On that night the king could not sleep. And he gave orders to bring the book of memorable deeds, the chronicles, and they were read before the king. And it was found written how Mordecai had told about Bigthana and Teresh, two of the king's eunuchs, who guarded the threshold, and who had sought to lay hands on King Ahasuerus. And the king said, "What honor or distinction has been bestowed on Mordecai for this?" The king's young men who attended him said, "Nothing has been done for him."

(Esther 6:1-3)

THERE ARE TIMES in life where it can be really hard to tell what God is doing. Sometimes we think we know what God is doing, and then all of the sudden, things don't turn out the way we thought they were going to. Sometimes we think that we can see the end of a difficult season in life, and then just when we thought we were out of the woods, something else bad happens. A lot of bad things happen to us in life that just don't seem to make any sense.

The book of Esther is full of bad things happening that don't seem to make any sense. Mordecai saves the king's life, but his enemy Haman is made the second most powerful man in the empire. Then Haman talks the king into making a decree to destroy and kill and annihilate all the Jews in the world.

Fortunately, the Jews have someone on the inside since the queen happens to be Jewish. Unfortunately, she has hidden her true identity from the king. However, Esther decides that she will trust God and risk her life by going before the king and telling him the truth and pleading with him on behalf of her people. Chapter 4 comes to a climactic end with Esther saying, ". . . I will go to the king, though it is against the law, and if I perish, I perish" (Esther 4:16b).

The tension in this story seems to be at an all-time high. However, with Esther deciding to trust God and risk her life, resolution seems to be just around the corner. In other words, if God is going to show up, then you would certainly expect Him to show up here. So let's see what happens.

The day comes, and Esther puts on her royal robes and makes her way to the inner court of the king's palace. She turns the corner and sees the king holding his scepter and sitting on his royal throne. She stands there silently, holding her breath as she waits for him to notice her. The king looks up and sees her.

In Esther 5:2, we read, "And when the king saw Queen Esther standing in the court, she won favor in his sight, and he held out to Esther the golden scepter that was in his hand. Then Esther approached and touched the tip of the scepter."

She made it! Phase one is complete: she doesn't die! But now what? How is Esther going to bring up her request? After Esther touches his scepter, the king breaks the silence by saying, "What is it, Queen Esther? What is your request? It will be given you, even to the half of my kingdom" (Esther 5:3). There it is. Can you believe it! Not only does the king want to see her, but he promises to grant her whatever she asks for.

Honestly, things couldn't be better. It seems like God has gone before her, and now all she has to do is tell the king everything. Finally, the resolution that we have been waiting for.

So in verse 4, Esther says, "If it please the king, let the king and Haman come today to a feast that I have prepared for the king."

What? What just happened? The king promises Esther anything she can ask for, and she says, "Will you and Haman come to a feast?" What is going on?

Before we have time to figure out what is happening, the king has agreed, and the three of them are all drinking wine together at the feast.

Again, the king says to Esther, "What is your wish? It shall be granted you. And what is your request? Even to the half of the kingdom, it shall be fulfilled" (Esther 5:6). I guess maybe Esther knows what she is doing. So, now the moment is right—now that the king has had a little to drink, and they have had time to get reacquainted. This time, Esther says to him,

> "My wish and my request is: If I have found favor in the sight of the king, and if it please the king to grant my wish and fulfill my request, let the king and Haman come to the feast that I will prepare for them, and tomorrow I will do as the king has said." (Esther 5:7b-8)

Providence

Again Esther waits. Is she just putting it off because she is scared, or does she have some plan that we don't know about? Is she passing up a golden opportunity that she will later regret, or will tomorrow be a better time for her to tell the king her secret? The resolution we were waiting for continues to elude us as we realize that we are going to have to wait for tomorrow's feast.

With the tension this high, you would expect the next scene to be tomorrow's feast. I mean, what could possibly happen in the next 24 hours that could significantly add to this story?

But instead of skipping to tomorrow's feast, the author tells us that Haman went out that day, "Joyful and glad of heart" (Esther 5:9a). Of course it's hard for this to hold our interest when what we really want to hear about is tomorrow's feast.

But verse 9 goes on to say, "But when Haman saw Mordecai in the king's gate, that he neither rose nor trembled before him, he was filled with wrath against Mordecai."

Oh, no. Just when we thought the tension couldn't get worse, Haman runs into Mordecai again. Knowing just how wicked Haman is, we wonder how he is going to respond to this new development. Last time Mordecai refused to bow to Haman, Haman wrote a law condemning the entire Jewish race to certain death.

Verse 10 says, "Nevertheless, Haman restrained himself and went home, and he sent and brought his friends and his wife Zeresh." It seems like the author has raised the tension just to let it out again, and our minds go back to wondering about tomorrow's feast.

96

However, the author continues to tell us about Haman. He writes,

> And Haman recounted to them the splendor of his riches, the number of his sons, all the promotions with which the king had honored him, and how he had advanced him above the officials and the servants of the king. Then Haman said, "Even Queen Esther let no one but me come with the king to the feast she prepared. And tomorrow also I am invited by her together with the king. Yet all this is worth nothing to me, so long as I see Mordecai the Jew sitting at the king's gate." (Esther 5:11-13)

This whole section leaves us shaking our heads. I mean, how ridiculous can Haman be? First he gathers his friends around him in order to brag about everything he has, and then he ends by telling them that everything he has been bragging about doesn't mean a thing as long as Mordecai the Jew continues to sit at the king's gate. This passage reminds us about just how foolish Haman is and it makes us wonder how he ever got so much power. How could God possibly let such a foolish and wicked man have so much control over his people? Why is Haman taking center stage in a book of the Bible where God is supposed to be the hero? At this point, we are shaking our heads, assuming that this interlude is just to remind us what a fool Haman is.

But the next verse says,

> Then his wife Zeresh and all his friends said to him, "Let a gallows fifty cubits high be made, and in the morning

> tell the king to have Mordecai hanged upon it. Then go joyfully with the king to the feast." The idea pleased Haman, and he had the gallows made. (Esther 5:14-15)

This verse comes and seems to knock the wind out of us. Just when we're shaking our heads at Haman because he seems so foolish, the author brings us back to the reality that this fool is the second-most powerful person in the world. This whole time, we have been focused on what is going to happen at tomorrow's feast, and now we realize that Mordecai might not be alive by the time the feast takes place.

Esther put off telling the king her secret, and now it seems like that was a horrible miscalculation. Now it seems that while Esther is busy preparing her feast for Haman and the King tomorrow, the man who raised her will be impaled and raised up on a 75-foot stake.

At this point, it's difficult to see how this isn't going to happen. Haman is so confident that it's going to happen that he has his servants work all night to build a 75-foot stake in his backyard. Esther and Mordecai don't know anything about Haman's plan, so neither one of them is going to be of any help to stop it.

We began this chapter believing that God would show up and bring resolution. We thought that God would use Esther's bravery to put an end to all of Haman's evil plans. But that's not what happened. God didn't show up the way we thought He would, and Esther put off telling her secret; so now things have gone from bad to worse. It seems clear that nothing short of a miracle can save Mordecai now, and so far in the book of Esther, we haven't seen any miracles.

Does this sound familiar? How many of you feel like your life sometimes reads like the book of Esther? Sometimes bad things happen to us that we don't understand, right? Sometimes we think we see the resolution we long for, only to find out that things are actually worse than we thought. Sometimes things can feel so out of control that we wonder how God could possibly bring them back; so wrong that we wonder how they could ever be set right; so lost that we doubt that they could ever be restored. Sometimes in life we honestly don't understand what God is doing.

Let's be real. If we stopped the story right here, no wise man or pastor or counselor would be able to explain why these things are happening. At this point in the story,

- we don't see God's hand.
- it seems like Haman has more control over the fate of God's people than God does.
- the only people who have been working for good are asleep and unaware of the danger that they are in.
- we don't understand why God has allowed the things that He has allowed.

But the story isn't over. So let's continue on and see if God really is in control and if He really is able to keep all of His promises.

Since chapter 5 ends with night falling, we assume chapter 6 will begin in the morning with Haman coming to talk to the king.

But it doesn't. Instead we read, "On that night the king could not sleep" (Esther 6:1a). On that night—the night that the stake was being built to impale Mordecai on—the king couldn't sleep. What is the king of Persia going to do when he can't sleep? You might expect him to call for some beautiful women to entertain him. You might think he is hungry and will call for the cooks to make him a feast. Or go for a walk, or even work on some official government business that he needs to catch up on. As the king, he has millions of options at his disposal. So what does he do?

Verse 1b says, "And he gave orders to bring the book of memorable deeds, the chronicles, and they were read before the king." These are not riveting books of history; they are more like spreadsheets with the dates, events, names, and outcomes. Most scholars who have read ancient chronicles like this can attest to their dullness. Some people think the reason he has them read is because they are so boring they should put him to sleep.

Well, it doesn't work. In fact, as the hours pass and dawn approaches, the king is still awake, and the book is still being read. Verse 2 says, "And it was found written how Mordecai had told about Bigthana and Teresh, two of the king's eunuchs, who guarded the threshold, and who had sought to lay hands on King Ahasuerus."

So as Haman's servants are completing a 75-foot stake to impale Mordecai on, the king's servants happen to be reading about how Mordecai saved the king's life over four years ago. Actually, as the story of Mordecai is being read to the king, Haman is at that very moment awake and making his way excitedly to the palace to get the king's permission to kill Mordecai.

Of all the stories read to the king that night, this one catches his attention, and he says to his servant in verse 3: "What honor or distinction has been bestowed on Mordecai for this?" The king's attendant responds, "Nothing has been done for him."

This would have absolutely shocked the king. Persian kings were famous for generously rewarding people for their service. They took pride in rewarding good deeds because they knew how important it was to keep up morale and encourage loyalty. In one historical book, we find that when someone saved the life of the king's brother, he was made governor of an entire province; but here Mordecai had saved the king's life with no subsequent reward.

The king jumps out of bed in order to make this the first project of the day. But this king (as we have seen) always needs advice, so he says to his servant, "Who is in the court?" On any other day, the court would be empty this early; but this morning is different.

Verse 4b says, "Now Haman had just entered the outer court of the king's palace to speak to the king about having Mordecai hanged on the gallows that he had prepared for him."

Of course Haman knows it is early, and he probably assumes he will have to wait for a while before he will be able to talk to the king. But he wants to make sure he is first in line when the time comes. Haman has seen the finished stake towering above the city, and he can't wait to have Mordecai impaled on it. When the king's men see Haman enter the court, they tell the king in verse 5b, "Haman is there, standing in the court."

Now the king is excited to hear that Haman is there because he doesn't have any idea what to do for Mordecai. And Haman is excited because he can't believe that the king is already up and wanting to see him. So Haman comes in, having already rehearsed everything he wants to say; but before he can say a word, the king interrupts his thoughts by asking him, "What should be done to the man whom the king delights to honor?" (Esther 6:6b).

The king's question takes Haman completely by surprise. He had come in, focused on getting revenge. However, the king's question has taken his mind off of revenge and placed it on the only thing he likes talking about more than revenge: himself.

Verse 6c says, "Haman said to himself 'Whom would the king delight to honor more than me?'" The irony of what is happening here is unbelievable, isn't it? Haman comes in wanting to kill and publicly shame Mordecai while the king wants to honor Mordecai; however, because the king does not mention Mordecai's name, Haman thinks that the king wants to honor him.

Notice how Haman responds: "For the man whom the king delights to honor . . ." He pauses as if he needs to think about how to respond. This is the moment he has been dreaming of all his life. As he begins to speak, he is picturing each of these things being done to him and savoring every word:

> "[L]et royal robes be brought, which the king has worn, and the horse that the king has ridden, and on whose head a royal crown is set. And let the robes and the horse be handed over to one of the king's most noble officials. Let them dress the man whom the king delights to honor, and let them lead him on the horse through the square of the city, proclaiming before him: 'Thus shall it be done to the man whom the king delights to honor.'" (Esther 6:8-9)

Haman is caught in a dream world. Notice his favorite line, the one that he repeats three times: "The man the king delights to honor." Haman loves thinking about himself and saying that line, because it is all he has ever longed for—to be the man the king delights to honor.

The king wakes Haman from his daydream by saying, "Hurry; take the robes and the horse, as you have said, and do so to Mordecai the Jew, who sits at the king's gate. Leave out nothing that you have mentioned" (Esther 6:10b).

Can you fathom this scene? Can you imagine the massive reversal that has just taken place that only Haman is fully aware of? You see, only Haman knows that there is a 75-foot stake looking down on the entire city, which he was planning on impaling Mordecai the Jew on. Only Haman knows that all night long, he has been salivating over seeing Mordecai shamed before the entire city. Now instead of seeing his enemy shamed, Haman will have to watch his enemy receive the very honor that he had spent his entire life longing for.

And of course, he doesn't just have to watch these things; he actually has to be the one to lead the horse through the city. That line that he once enjoyed saying so much has become the most difficult thing in all of the world for him to say. And yet over and over again, he has to shout out about his worst enemy, "Thus shall it be done to the man the king delights to honor!" In one moment, Haman's greatest dream has turned into his worst nightmare.

When it is all over, verse 12 says, "Then Mordecai returned to the king's gate. But Haman hurried to his house, mourning and with his head covered."

Providence

After three days of fasting, the Jewish people have stopped mourning and returned to work. And on the fourth day:

- Mordecai, instead of being impaled on a stake, is dressed in the king's robes and led through the city by his greatest enemy.
- Haman, the enemy of the Jews, ends up being the one who is mourning and covering his face in shame.

This reversal of fortunes exceeds anything we could imagine, and it functions as the turning point of the entire book of Esther.

It seemed like Esther's going before the king would be the turning point; but as we have seen, even after the king agreed to Esther's request, things continued to get worse. However, after what takes place in chapter 6, even Haman's wife and friends know that the tables have turned. Listen to what they say in verse 13:

> And Haman told his wife Zeresh and all his friends everything that had happened to him. Then his wise men and his wife Zeresh said to him, "If Mordecai, before whom you have begun to fall, is of the Jewish people, you will not overcome him but will surely fall before him."

Who is responsible for this great reversal of fortunes?

We assumed that Esther or Mordecai would be the hero of this story, but both of them are fast asleep when everything begins to change. Consider these questions:

- Whose wisdom or courage or cunning is responsible for what takes place in this chapter?
- Whose plan is being executed?
- Who should get the glory for what takes place here?
- Who keeps the king awake on this of all nights?
- Why does the king decide to read the book of remembrances, and how is it that he just happens to read through a story that took place more four years ago?
- How is it that a Persian king has forgotten to reward the man who saved his life?
- How is it that Haman happens to be in the court at the exact moment that the king is looking for advice?
- Why does the king neglect to mention that Mordecai was the one he wanted to honor?
- What was it about Haman that makes him so quick to assume the king is talking about him?
- Why does he ask that it be one of the king's most noble officials who carries out this task, instead of one of his servants?

Do you see how none of these things in and of themselves seem impossible or even out of character—and yet, put together, they scream of someone behind the scenes? Whoever made up this plan has been patiently working on it for a long time.

Of course, the answer to all these questions is, "God." God is the One Who has been working behind the scenes on this plan for years. The word that theologians use for what we see in this chapter is, "Providence." Providence is, "the way that God directs the flow of human history through the ordinary lives of individuals to fulfill His promises."

You and I thought the only thing that could save Mordecai was a miracle. What we didn't understand was that God is so powerful that He is able to save Mordecai without resorting to the supernatural.

God is the Hero of the book of Esther even though He does all His work behind the scenes. God is the One Who has been orchestrating these events from the very beginning—without doing any violence to human responsibility. Each character in this book does what they want to do, and yet God orchestrates it all in order to fulfill His promises.

God is the Hero of the book of Esther even though He does all His work behind the scenes.

From within the story, you can't see what God is doing. From within the story, bad things just look bad, period. Only later are we able to see how God has taken these bad things and used them for His glory and for the good of His people.

From within the story, it seems to Mordecai that he has been cheated; that instead of being rewarded for saving the king's life, his enemy has been rewarded for no good reason. It seems to him that the king has forgotten about him. Not only does he not receive a reward, but soon he finds out that the king has condemned every Jew in the empire to death.

From within the story, this only looks bad. From Mordecai's perspective, it must seem like even God has forgotten him, and doing the right thing probably doesn't seem to be worth it. But what Mordecai doesn't know is that God has a plan.

God hasn't forgotten about Mordecai; instead, He has been waiting to give him his reward until the day that He knew it would be most needed. God knew that one day, one of Mordecai's enemies would build a 75-foot stake in his backyard and wake up early in the morning to ask the king to impale Mordecai on it. And God decided that He would wait until then to have the king give Mordecai his reward.

God holds all the cards, and God knows when to play them. Mordecai would have played his reward card much earlier if he were holding it. But God knows the future, and He knew exactly when this card would be necessary. So He waits for just the right moment, and as we look back on the story, we can all admit that God's timing couldn't have been better.

APPLICATION

So, what would it look like for you to apply these truths to your own life? Where are you having a hard time seeing what God is doing? Where have you been waiting for God to show up, but it seems like He is nowhere to be found? What cards does God hold that you think He should have already played? In what areas of your life do you feel like God has forgotten you? What parts of your life seem unfair?

We typically don't mind trusting God as long as we understand what He is doing; if He will show us how He plans to use something bad in our life for good, then usually we will trust

Providence

Him. Isn't that why we are always trying to figure out what God is doing? We desperately want to understand how God plans to use the bad things in our lives for good. When we can't figure it out, we ask others what they think; but until we get an answer that we can agree with, we often find ourselves paralyzed to move forward.

But that isn't the way it should work. God doesn't tell Mordecai why the king forgot about him; He doesn't tell Mordecai why He let the king make a decree to kill all the Jews; He doesn't tell Mordecai why any of these things happened. Nobody in the story knows why they are happening. But God calls Mordecai to believe that regardless of how bleak things might appear, God will keep His promises.

In John 13:7b, Jesus says to Peter, "What I am doing you do not understand now, but afterward you will understand." That is the kind of faith that God is calling us to have—the kind that says, "Even though I don't understand why God is letting this happen, I know one day I will understand; so right now, I am going to trust Him."

There will be times in your story that you don't see what God is doing, times where it doesn't seem like there is anything in the world that God could do in order to keep His promises. And even though you might ask your pastor or your friends, there will be times when they don't know either. That is the way God designed the world. Bad things look bad from within the story. Bad things can even look unredeemable from within the story.

But know this: your God has a plan to use even the bad things in this world and in your life for the good of everyone who puts their faith in Him (Romans 8:28). He holds the cards, and He will play each card at just the right time. Right now, you don't understand; but one day, you will.

When that day comes, you will be glad for every moment that you chose to put your trust in God. No one who puts their trust in Him will ever be put to shame (Romans 9:33). One day, our God will fix everything that is broken, and He will keep all of His precious and very great promises.

How do I know this? How do I know for certain that God is strong enough to fix all that is broken and that He loves us enough to keep every promise? Because the book of Esther, with its massive reversals and intricately laid plans that take years to unfold, is actually only a shadow of a much bigger story with a much more intricate plan that took much longer to unfold.

In the first few pages of the Bible, we get our first glimpse of this plan—one that would require a perfect Hero to be born from one of Eve's offspring, and to somehow have the power to conquer sin and death and ultimately to crush the head of the devil himself. But everything doesn't always run smoothly.

The Bible contains story after story about the obstacles that needed to be overcome to bring this Hero into the world:

- Barren women give birth.
- Enslaved people are rescued from the most powerful nation in the world.
- Time and again, God shows patience to a rebellious and stiff-necked people.
- Hero after hero is born, but each fails to live up to God's standard and is unable to truly rescue God's people.
- For 400 years, no one hears a word from this God.

Providence

Then at just the right time, God sends his only Son, placing Him in the womb of a virgin to be born as a tiny baby.

Unlike every other hero, this Hero—Jesus—is born without sin. Almost immediately, the Hero is in danger as King Herod sends his soldiers to try to kill Him. Jesus escapes to Egypt and then grows up in Nazareth. At about the age of 30, He finally begins to reveal Himself to the world. So he gathers some disciples around Him and begins to tour the country, healing people and raising people from the dead and teaching them about the kingdom of God.

Finally one Sunday afternoon, He gets on a donkey and rides into Jerusalem, and the crowds proclaim Him King. After all these years, the Messiah has finally come. Everyone is excited to see how He will free them from Rome and set up His kingdom.

Then over the course of one night, everything changes. One of His disciples betrays Him, and another denies Him. The religious leaders capture Him, and a political leader condemns Him. Before you know it, the Hero Who was supposed to crush Satan's head, is hanging helplessly from a Roman cross.

Unlike in Esther, where the hero goes from a death sentence to a parade through the city in the nick of time, this Hero goes from a parade through the city to a death sentence and ends up on a cross.

No one had seen this coming! The disciples lock themselves in a room for fear of the Jews, and His followers mourn because they had hoped that Jesus was the One. They had thought that He was the Hero promised to Eve, that He was going to save them; instead, His body lay lifeless in a borrowed tomb.

But you remember who holds the cards, right? And you remember you can't always understand the story until it's over? Even though Jesus is dead, the story isn't over; God has a card left to play: the resurrection card. On the third day, He plays His card, rolls the stone away from the tomb, and raises His Son Jesus up from the dead. Then He gives Him a name above every name in all the universe (Philippians 2:9). That is how God treats the Man Whom He delights to honor.

Now because God raised Jesus from the dead, anyone who believes in Him doesn't have to be scared of death anymore; instead, His people can know that Jesus has conquered sin and death and Satan, and that He is able to save anyone who puts their trust in Him.

I don't know what struggles you are facing today. I don't know what parts of your story seem confusing right now. I don't know where you are having a hard time finding hope. But this is what I do know: there is a God Who loved His people so much that He gave His only Son on the cross to forgive them of all their sins (John 3:16).

God loves you, and He will not leave you alone in your suffering. He is powerful enough to overcome any obstacle that you might be facing.

This God loves you. He loves you, and He will not leave you alone in your suffering. He is the One holding all the cards, and if He is powerful enough to raise His Son from the dead, you can

Providence

know that He is powerful enough to overcome any obstacle that you might be facing. The God Who used the cross to bring us our salvation is able to take all the bad, all the evil, and all the unexplainable suffering you have ever endured, and use it for your eternal good.

The God Who did not spare His own Son is going to keep all His promises. You may not see Him at work, but He is. You may not understand what He is doing, but He has a plan. Won't you trust Him? Won't you stop clinging to control of your life and instead look to Jesus? Right now, you may not understand what He is doing; but I promise that one day, you will. So until then, won't you trust Him?

CHAPTER 7: LIFE & DEATH

Text: Esther 7

Then Queen Esther answered, "If I have found
favor in your sight, O king, and if it please the
king, let my life be granted me for my wish, and
my people for my request. For we have been sold,
I and my people, to be destroyed, to be killed,
and to be annihilated. . . ."

(Esther 7:3-4a)

WHO GETS LIFE? Who gets death? In Esther chapter 7,
two people sit down for a feast with the king of
Persia, and both of them end up pleading for their
lives. One is executed, and the other is saved.

Have you ever had something that you really felt like you
needed to tell someone, but you were afraid about how they would
react? It feels like the timing is never right, and so you keep
waiting. But the longer you wait, the more awkward it feels to try
to bring it up.

Well, that is how Esther feels. For five years, she has been
keeping her Jewish identity a secret from the king; but today is
the day that she plans to tell him. Normally, it might not have
been that big of a deal; but since the king passed a law that all

Jews are to be killed, Esther is very nervous about how he will respond to her little secret.

Maybe it would help you understand the situation if I told you about another guy who happened to ask King Ahasuerus for a favor. History tells us that there was a man who had given King Ahasuerus a large sum of money to help him fight against the Greeks. This same man had also entertained the king in his own home on a number of occasions. All five of his sons were in the army and were preparing for war. This man really wanted to pass on his family name, so he asked the king if he would release his eldest son from military duty. After all that he had done for the king, he didn't think that this would be too much to ask. Do you know how the king answered this man's request? He took the eldest son, the one this man had wanted released so badly, and cut him in half with a sword. Then he had his army walk in between the two pieces of this young man's body.

That is the kind of man that Esther is married to. This is the man that she is about to tell her secret to. So why does she do it? What could possibly convince her to risk her life by telling the king that she is Jewish?

Esther has taken Mordecai's words to heart and has come to believe that the safest place for her in all of the world is to be identified with God's people. Safer than the palace, safer than being the wife of the most powerful man in the world, safer than all of these places—is being one of God's people.

God had made some amazing promises to His people. He had promised His people that He would be their God and that they would be His people (Exodus 6:7). He had promised that He would ultimately bless them and curse all those who rose up against them (Genesis 12:1-3). And so, because Esther believes these promises, she chooses to risk her life by aligning herself with God's people and clinging to His promises.

That is why she risked her life to appear before the king, why she intends to tell the king her secret.

Can you imagine how Esther is feeling as she rehearses her lines in her head? Her heart is pounding as she waits for the right time to address the king. The time comes. In Esther 7:2, we read, "As they were drinking wine after the feast, the king again said to Esther, 'What is your wish, Queen Esther? It shall be granted you. And what is your request? Even to the half of my kingdom, it shall be fulfilled.'"

The king is probably thinking that Esther may want a new room addition in the palace, maybe some new outfits, a horse, or a summer vacation. People always seem to be asking him for stuff, and he likes making a big scene about giving it to them.

Esther begins very respectfully by saying in verse 3, "If I have found favor in your sight, O king, and if it please the king . . ." The king must appreciate how respectful Esther is. She is nothing like his first wife.

Esther continues, ". . . if it please the king, let my life be granted me for my wish, and my people for my request . . ." Notice how the king has offered her both a wish and a request, so she is prepared for both.

Can you imagine how this must have perked the king's attention? He must have been thinking, "Your life is your wish? What do you mean, what are you talking about? Is your life in some sort of danger? Is someone trying to kill you? And did you say, 'The life of your people' is your request? What's going on?

Who are your people anyway? I guess I never got around to asking you about them (my bad); but now that you mention them, are they in some sort of trouble?"

Esther has certainly gotten the king's attention. Knowing this, she continues, "We have been sold, I and my people, to be destroyed, to be killed, and to be annihilated" (Esther 7:4).

What? The king has got to be wracking his brain, trying to understand what she is talking about. Who would do such a thing? Who would dare to insult the throne by threatening the queen and her people? The king is probably starting to get really angry, but he doesn't know yet who he is supposed to be angry with.

And then, very respectfully, Esther says, "If we had been sold merely as slaves, men and women, I would have been silent, for our affliction is not to be compared with the loss to the king" (Esther 7:4).

Notice how sweet she is. To paraphrase: "If someone sold me into slavery, I wouldn't bother you. It's just that they want to kill and destroy and annihilate me and all of my people; that's the only reason that I am even bringing this up."

The king is furious now. A threat against the queen is an affront on his empire, and it is disrespectful to the throne. The king can't fathom how anyone could do something like that. Plus, Esther is such a sweet person. Who would want to hurt her?

The king responds by saying, "Who is he, and where is he, who has dared to do this?" (Esther 7:5b). Notice what Esther has done. The way she has told the story has aroused the king's anger before he even knows who he is angry with.

Let's imagine this conversation if Esther would have approached it differently.

Esther: Do you want to know what my request is? Oh honey, I will tell you what it is. You and Haman made a law to kill and destroy all of the Jews. Well, guess what? I am Jewish. Now why would you go and make a law like that?

King: You're Jewish? Why didn't you tell me?

Esther: Well, I didn't think you were interested. You never even asked. Anyway, don't turn this on me. You're the one who made a law to kill an entire race of people without even knowing what race your wife is.

You see, if she had gone about it that way, she probably would have been the one getting killed. But this way, the king is furious, and he still doesn't even know who he is angry with. Once Esther points the finger, she knows she won't be able to take it back.

So when the king asks her, "Who is he, and where is he, who has dared to do this?" Esther points her finger and says, "A foe and enemy! This wicked Haman!" (Esther 7:6b).

I want you to think about how fast this all must have taken place. Haman is sitting there enjoying a meal with the king and queen. The king asks the queen what she wants, and Haman assumes she wants some ridiculous trinket or something. Before he can figure out what is happening, he is listening as Esther repeats the exact wording that he put in the law to kill the Jews. He notices that the king's face is turning red with anger. Then the king shouts out, "Who is he, and where is he!" and Esther looks at Haman and points at him and says, "A foe and enemy! This wicked Haman!" Verse 7a tells us, "The king arose in his wrath from the wine-drinking and went into the palace garden . . ." And Haman is left there absolutely stunned.

What just happened? A second ago, he was feeling on top of the world as he enjoyed an intimate dinner with the king and queen. Then literally in a matter of moments, the queen is pointing at him, and he can tell from the king's face that his life is over.

Haman at this point has three options:

1. **Go to the king in the garden.** But that doesn't sound like a very good idea, considering the state the king is in right now.
2. **Go somewhere else.** But then the king will think he is guilty and will probably make up some reason to get rid of him.
3. **Plead with the queen.** But technically it's against harem protocol for a man to be within seven steps of the queen or to speak with her without the king present.

With no good option out there, Haman decides to stay with the queen and plead for his life.

The king, meanwhile, is out in the garden trying to figure out what to do. We don't know what conclusion he comes to, but we can safely assume he is brainstorming how he can save face in this situation. He is trying to figure out how he can save his wife and punish Haman without looking bad. After all, he is the one who gave Haman permission to make that law.

Fortunately, Haman makes the king's decision easy. The king returns and finds Haman falling before the queen and pleading with her for his life—in direct violation of palace laws. The king exclaims in verse 8b, "Will he even assault the queen in my presence, in my own house?" The chapter continues:

> As the word left the mouth of the king, they covered Haman's face. Then Harbona, one of the eunuchs in attendance on the king, said, "Moreover, the gallows that Haman has prepared for Mordecai, whose word saved the king, is standing at Haman's house, fifty cubits high." And the king said, "Hang him on that." So they hanged Haman on the gallows that he had prepared for Mordecai. Then the wrath of the king abated. (Esther 7:8c-10)

The end of this story emphasizes the great reversal that has just taken place. Haman is impaled on the very stake that he built in his own backyard to kill Mordecai on.

Consider for a moment just how quick and how complete Haman's demise is. Earlier that same day, when the king had asked him, "What should be done to the man the king delights to honor?" Haman had thought, "Whom would the king delight to honor more than me?" Now less than a day later, his face is covered, and he is impaled on the very stake he built to shame his enemy.

In this story, Haman learns just how suddenly death can come. Haman never sees his death coming. He had always believed that his wealth and his position of power and his personal relationship with the king would keep him safe from death; but he is wrong. Because he has always felt safe, Haman isn't ready to die. That is why this proud man falls at the feet of a Jewish woman to plead for his life. He isn't ready to die, and he is willing to do whatever it takes to avoid it.

What about you? Are you ready for death? Or, like Haman, do you feel safe? Do you feel like death is a long way off? Do you feel like there will be plenty of time to prepare for it later? The reality is that all of us are going to die, and some of us will certainly die unexpectedly. The question is, will we be ready?

Because Haman wasn't ready, death stole from him everything that he had lived for. The man who lived to be seen by others as significant and important was impaled 75 feet high, for all the city to see. The man who bragged about having ten sons died in shame right outside of their bedroom windows. In chapter 8, we will see that all of Haman's possessions are given to his archenemy Mordecai. Truly when death came for Haman, it stole from him everything he had ever lived for.

What about you? What are you living for? Where do you seek your happiness? What are you putting your hope in? Are you living for things that will last, or will death one day come and steal everything from you as well?

If we were honest, most of us would have to admit we have spent much of our lives living for things that won't last. Like Haman, we have spent our lives collecting things we can't take with us. We have chosen to build our lives around our careers or our families or our comfort or pleasure.

Like Haman, we have lived for our glory instead of for the glory of the God who made us. We have followed our feelings instead of submitting to His perfect word. We have done everything we could to make ourselves the center instead of joyfully worshiping the true God.

When Haman realizes his mistake, he begs Queen Esther to save him. But Esther doesn't save him. Esther knows that the king is angry, and she knows that someone will have to die before his anger is satisfied. So, because Haman deserves it, and because she longs to live, she lets the king take his wrath out on Haman.

When Haman saw the king's anger, he looked around desperately for a savior, but he didn't find one. I want you to know that your story can be different.

APPLICATION

The Bible tells us that there is another Savior Who is even better than Esther. Esther risked her life in order to save herself and her people, but the Bible tells us that Jesus gave His life in order to save His enemies.

Like Esther, Jesus left His throne in order to identify with His people. But even though He came to His own people, the Bible tells us that His people didn't receive Him (John 1:11). Instead, His people actually called out for Him to be crucified.

Esther risked her life to save her people, but Jesus gave His life to save His enemies.

I want you to consider for a moment how angry God the Father must have been by the way people treated His only Son. If King Ahasuerus was angry when someone threatened his wife, how do you think God the Father felt when people abused His only Son? How do you think He felt when people called out for His crucifixion?

Do you know that the Romans wouldn't even crucify the worst Roman citizen in the world? They thought that being a Roman citizen made you above being crucified. It didn't matter what you did; the idea of crucifying a Roman citizen was seen as ridiculous. So how do you think God felt when He watched the people He had created think that it was somehow okay to crucify His only Son? I will tell you how he felt. He felt angry. He felt angry like King Ahasuerus was angry when his wife was threatened.

But notice what Jesus did. He did not call out to his Father and say, "Look, Father, an enemy and a foe! Destroy these people who have sought to destroy me." Instead, He said, "Father forgive them . . ." (Luke 23:34b). When God had all His anger against His people's sin pent up, Jesus chose not to point His finger. Instead, Jesus stepped up and willingly took all of God's anger against His people's sin upon Himself. When He said, "It is finished," He meant that He had taken in His body on the cross all of God's anger at His people so that now the wrath of God is abated.

Here is what that means for us today: It's not too late. Yes, we are sinners; yes, our sin has earned us the wrath of the King. But it's not too late for us, because Jesus is a better Savior than Esther. And if you will fall at His feet, then He will take your place.

Listen to how the author of Hebrews says it:

> Because God's children are human beings—made of flesh and blood—the Son also became flesh and blood. For only as a human being could he die, and only by dying could he break the power of the devil, who had the power of

death. Only in this way could he set free all who have lived their lives as slaves to the fear of dying. (Hebrews 2:14-15, NLT)

You and I don't have to be afraid of death anymore. Our Savior Who is better than Esther took on flesh and died our death so that He might set us free.

In Acts 2:36-37, we see an amazing picture of how this works. Peter says,

> Let all the house of Israel therefore know for certain that God has made him both Lord and Christ, this Jesus whom you crucified. Now when they heard this, they were cut to the heart, and said to Peter and the rest of the apostles, "Brothers, what shall we do?"

Peter points to them and says, "You crucified Jesus. Jesus, the Son of God—Jesus the Lord and the Christ—that is the One you crucified." And when the audience hears this, they are cut to the quick and realize how angry God must be at them. They realize how much trouble they must be in. Like Haman, they know that God must intend to do them harm for the way they have treated His Son. And they say to Peter, "What shall we do?" They want to know if there is hope for people like them—hope for the people who crucified Jesus. And Peter says this: "Repent and be baptized every one of you in the name of Jesus Christ for the forgiveness of your sins, and you will receive the gift of the Holy Spirit" (Acts 2:38).

This is the Gospel. It is the good news that a wicked people who crucified God's only Son can be forgiven if they will only turn to Him in repentance. Some of you may wonder if it's possible for God to forgive you. Some of you may feel like you have gone too far or done too much to be forgiven. Listen to what Peter says. He says that even those who crucified Jesus can be forgiven. They can be forgiven because on the cross, Jesus bore God's wrath against His people. Jesus is better than Esther because, instead of clinging to His life, He willingly offered it up so that He might save His enemies.

So I beg you to turn to Him. I beg you to repent of your sins right now and look to Jesus. I want you to see what an amazing Savior you have.

Maybe you have known Him for years; I want you to see again just how amazing your Savior is. Maybe you have never truly come to Him; maybe you have never fallen at His feet and pled for your life. Either way, now is the time. This is the moment that you can repent of your sins and plead with Him for mercy. If you will do this, I promise you, He will forgive you.

Others of you may feel like you're not that bad and you don't really need a Savior. Just remember, that is exactly how Haman felt until he realized that his decree against the Jews was actually a decree against the wife of the king. One day, you will realize that all of your sin has actually been against the God Who made you. If you wait until death shows you that, it will be too late.

So please don't neglect God's amazing gift. Don't put this book down without knowing and loving and worshiping Jesus Who gave His life to offer you the forgiveness of your sins. We have the best Savior imaginable, so won't you worship Him now?

Chapter 8: Pride

Text: Esther 7

As the word left the mouth of the king, they covered Haman's face. Then Harbona, one of the eunuchs in attendance on the king, said, "Moreover, the gallows that Haman has prepared for Mordecai, whose word saved the king, is standing at Haman's house, fifty cubits high." And the king said, "Hang him on that." So they hanged Haman on the gallows that he had prepared for Mordecai.

(Esther 7:8b-10a)

IN 8TH GRADE, a new student joined our school. He was from Atlanta, Georgia, and his dad worked for the Coca-Cola Company. From the first day this kid came in, he was full of stories. He told us that his dad had the secret recipe for Coke, and that they would make it fresh every night in their basement. He would see someone open up a can of Coke during lunch, and he would laugh at him and tell us that once you have had a fresh Coke, you can't go back to the canned stuff. It didn't matter what story you had, Chip always had a story that was similar enough to tell, but way better. It didn't take long for us to figure out that Chip was pretty arrogant; everything was always about him.

There is something about arrogant people that seems to rub us wrong, isn't there? When you hear this story, or when you think about the word "Pride," do you have a name or a face that comes immediately to mind? We all know people whom we consider to be arrogant—people who always seem to be looking down on others; people who can make us feel judged simply by the way they look at us; people who always have to be the center of attention; people who always interrupt in order to tell their story or show off their knowledge.

Let's be honest, when it comes to pride, you and I are pretty good at spotting it in other people, aren't we?

C.S. Lewis had this to say about pride: "There is no fault which makes a man more unpopular, and no fault which we are more unconscious of in ourselves. And the more we have it ourselves, the more we dislike it in others."[11]

How do you feel about proud people? How do you feel when you think someone is judging you? How do you feel when you meet someone who clearly thinks that they are better than you? How do you feel when you see someone on a power trip? Lewis says the best way to tell if you are proud is to consider how other people's pride makes you feel. The more pride that you have, the more you will find yourself disliking it in others.

This has been a really sobering thought for me because I don't enjoy being around proud people. They rub me wrong. Do you know what I do after spending an evening with someone who

---

[11] C.S. Lewis, *Mere Christianity* (New York, NY: Macmillan Publishing Company, 1952), 109.

comes across really arrogant? I ask my wife if that is how other people see me. I ask her if I act like that. And if she says, "No," do you know what I do? I feel good about myself and am thankful that I don't come across like that person did.

Do you notice what I have done in that situation? I have just looked down on someone else because I thought they were proud. I have just felt good about myself because I thought that I was better than that person who came across so full of themselves.

Joseph Epstein says, "So many people hate snobs, but you can only hate snobs if you feel superior to them. And that is simply another form of snobbery."[12] Do you see the trap? Most of us probably look down on arrogant people, not realizing that in doing so, we are revealing our own form of pride.

Most of us probably look down on arrogant people, not realizing that in doing so we are revealing our own form of pride.

Tim Keller points out that one of the most dangerous things about pride is that it hides itself. He says, "By definition, the more proud you are, the less proud you think you are."[13]

This chapter is about pride. But I don't want you to be thinking about anyone else. Each of us has enough pride in our own lives to deal with, and we don't need to be distracted by other

---

[12] Quoted by Tim Keller, "The man the king delights to honor," sermon (April 29, 2007). sermons2.redeemer.com/sermons/man-king-delights-honor

[13] Tim Keller, "The man the king delights to honor," sermon (April 29, 2007).

Pride

people. C.S. Lewis said, "If anyone wants to acquire humility, you must realize that you are proud. Nothing can be done before this. If you think you are not conceited, it means you are very conceited indeed."[14] The only way for this topic to sink in is to take it personally.

In the Bible, the character of Haman is the most sustained case study that we have on pride. That's why, before we move on from Haman, I want to take one last look at his life to see what he can teach us about pride. As we look at Haman's life, we are going to see three themes:

1. What pride does
2. Where pride comes from
3. What pride leads to

WHAT PRIDE DOES

We first meet Haman in Esther 3 where we find that he has just been elevated to the second-most powerful position in the entire Persian Empire, and the king has commanded everyone to bow before him. However, Mordecai the Jew refuses to bow down. Verses 5-6 tells us Haman's reaction to this:

> And when Haman saw that Mordecai did not bow down or pay homage to him, Haman was filled with fury. But he disdained to lay hands on Mordecai alone. So, as they had made known to him the people of Mordecai, Haman sought to destroy all the Jews, the people of Mordecai, throughout the whole kingdom of Ahasuerus.

[14] Lewis, *Mere Christianity*, 114

Take a moment and process what is happening. In Esther 3, Mordecai refuses to bow down to Haman, and Haman's pride is so wounded that he decides the only way to make up for it is to destroy every single Jew in the entire empire. Haman wants to destroy millions and millions of people because Mordecai won't bow down to him. Now this sounds absolutely crazy, but this passage shows us what pride does.

Pride makes itself the center; in order to do that, it uses other people to build itself up. Notice how clearly we see this in Haman. Haman's pride leads him to think that the sole purpose of the Jews' existence is for him to use them to make him feel better about himself. Haman is willing to kill millions and millions of Jews as long as it makes him look better. That is what pride does: it makes us the center, and it uses people for our benefit.

We haven't tried to kill millions of people, but you and I have used people to make ourselves look or feel better, haven't we? You and I have made ourselves the center, and in our self-absorption, we have used other people for our benefit.

How many of us have ever judged people and used their failures to make us feel better about ourselves? That's what I do when I look at proud people and judge them; I use their failure to make me feel better about myself.

How many of us have ever talked about others' problems or gossiped about their sin because it made us feel better about our own lives? We may not have been trying to hurt them; we were simply using them for our own benefit without ever really considering their feelings.

Pride

How many of us want others to listen to us when we talk about our problems or our stories—and yet when others want to share their stories or talk about their struggles, we have a hard time being interested?

How many of us have ever felt jealous or critical of others when they get something that we really wish we had?

- Singles, have you ever seen someone start to date and thought that should be you? You have waited longer, you are more ready to date, and you are more focused on God than they are; so why do they get to date, and you are still single?
- Couples, have you ever heard of someone getting pregnant and thought that should be you? Why do they get kids, and you don't? What makes them think they are ready to be parents?
- Employees, how do you respond when someone else gets a promotion you want? Do you think, "Why did they get it? I work harder than they do, and I have been with the company longer than they have!"
- Church family, when someone gets asked to lead something at church, do you ever think, "Why did I get passed over? What do they see in him or her that they don't see in me? Don't they know I could do a better job?"

Whatever it is that you really value, you probably find it really hard to watch others get it—especially when you think you deserve it more.

But you see, that is pride. We want to be the center, so we make the good things happening in other people's lives about us. We make their promotion or their pregnancy or their big church about us instead of celebrating with them. All we can do is think that we are the ones who should have what they have.

Now that we have seen what pride is, let's take a second and see where pride comes from.

WHERE PRIDE COMES FROM

Because pride makes us the center and involves being self-absorbed, there are actually two forms of pride:

1. Pride of Superiority—where we compare ourselves to others and feel like we are better than they are.
2. Pride of Inferiority—where we compare ourselves to others and feel like we are failures and so constantly beat ourselves up.

I think we all understand the Pride of Superiority, so let me focus on the Pride of Inferiority for a moment. Of course, this form of pride appears on the surface to look like humility; but everything is still about us, and it still uses people. Instead of being able to rejoice with people's success, this form of pride chooses to focus instead on our own failure. Consider these examples:

- Someone does something well, and all we can think is how much better they are than we are.
- We mess something up, and all we can think about is what a failure we are, how we will never be of any use to

anyone, and how everyone would be better off without us.

- Someone tries to encourage us, and we make them feel like a fool because they don't realize how unworthy we actually are.

Instead of thinking we are the best and using others to feel better about ourselves, we believe we are the worst—and we use others to make us more aware of our failure.

The problem with both forms of pride is that they make everything about us, and they use people.

Humility, on the other hand, comes as we recognize that we are not the center; life isn't all about us. It's certainly not about how good we are, but it's also not about how horrible we are either—because life simply isn't ultimately about us. We are not the center.

If you want to better understand what this humility would look like, consider the way C.S. Lewis describes it. He says humility is,

> . . . the state of mind where someone could build the best cathedral in the world, and know it was the best, and rejoice in it being the best without being any more or less or otherwise glad at having built it than if someone else had built it.[15]

Keller says, "Humility isn't thinking less about yourself; but it's thinking about yourself less."[16]

---

[15] C.S. Lewis, *The Screwtape Letters* (A Mentor Book, 1988), 55.

WHAT PRIDE LEADS TO

The problem with pride is that when we try to make ourselves the center, we end up losing, because there is One Who is already the center, and Isaiah tells us that He is not interested in sharing His glory with anyone else. In I Peter 5:5b, we read, "God opposes the proud but gives grace to the humble." God opposes the proud. He thwarts their plans. He keeps them always on the outside fighting for something they will never achieve. Proverbs 16:18a tells us that ultimately, "Pride goes before destruction."

That is what we see in the story of Esther. Haman is the second-most powerful person in the empire, and he builds a 75-foot stake in order to kill a Jewish man who has broken the king's law to bow before him. It seems like nothing can stop his plan. But God opposes the proud. So the next day, when Haman goes to ask the king to let him kill Mordecai, the king orders him to honor Mordecai instead. But that's not all. Read what happens next:

> Then Harbona, one of the eunuchs in attendance on the king, said, "Moreover, the gallows that Haman has prepared for Mordecai, whose word saved the king, is standing at Haman's house, fifty cubits high." And the king said, "Hang him on that." So they hanged Haman on the gallows that he had prepared for Mordecai. Then the wrath of the king abated. (Esther 7:9-10)

---

[16] Tim Keller, "The man the king delights to honor," sermon (April 29, 2007).

Haman ends up being impaled on the very stake that he had built for Mordecai. God opposes the proud.

APPLICATION

The truth is, there is no future for our pride. There is no future for our longing to be the center. Habakkuk 2:13-14 says, "Behold, is it not from the LORD of hosts that peoples labor merely for fire, and nations weary themselves for nothing? For the earth will be filled with the knowledge of the glory of the LORD as the waters cover the sea."

One day, the glory of the LORD will flood this world like a tsunami, and every tower of human pride will be crushed under its waves. There is simply no future for human pride.

So where does that leave us? Is there a future for people like us who have tried to be the center? Is there any hope for those of us who have used people like objects for our own benefit? Is it possible to find freedom from something that seems to be so much a part of who we are? If there were hope for people like us, where would we find it? What would it look like?

If Haman is the most sustained case study on pride in the Bible, then Jesus serves as the most sustained case study on humility. Jesus is the anti-Haman. In heaven, Jesus really was the center of the universe, and everything really did revolve around Him. If anyone had a right to use people for Himself, it was Jesus since He was the One Who had created them.

But instead of clinging to His glory and crushing all of our pride by coming down and sending us to the eternal destruction that our pride deserved, Jesus was different.

Jesus tells his disciples in Mark 10:45, "For even the Son of Man came not to be served but to serve, and to give His life as a ransom for many." Jesus—the true center—let go of being the center in order to show us what true humility looks like. Instead of using people for His good, He took on flesh and came to earth, where everything He did was for the good of His people.

How tempting must it have been for Jesus to act like He was the center of the universe? If you and I find it hard not to try to be the center of the universe, when it's so obvious that we are not, how much harder must it have been for Jesus to not act like the center of the universe, when He actually was?

Even though He could have demanded that each one of us bow before Him in humble service, Jesus chose to come and humbly serve us. Instead of using people, Jesus served people. On the last night of His life, when everything should have been about Him, He got up from the table and took off His outer garment and put a towel around His waist. He did what no superior in all of ancient literature had ever thought of doing: He washed His disciples' feet. He bent over and wiped the manure off of the feet of the man who he knew would soon betray Him.

The humblest man to ever walk the face of the earth was God.

Jesus willingly gave up the very thing that you and I are constantly trying to grasp. Though He was God, He didn't cling to His equality with God, but instead humbled Himself and took on the form of a servant (Philippians 2). Oh how different He is from us! Even though we are created human beings, we are constantly grasping after equality with God—which we don't deserve and will never achieve. While you and I are constantly stepping on other people trying to make ourselves higher than we really are, Jesus willingly left heaven and came all the way down to earth.

Jesus is nothing like us, and He was nothing like Haman. But what makes Jesus' story so mind-blowing is that even though He was nothing like Haman, He ended up dying the same sort of shameful death that Haman died. Haman's death makes sense, right? "Pride goes before destruction," so since Haman was so proud, you would expect to see him ultimately face destruction. But what about Jesus? How is it that Jesus ends up dying the same sort of shameful death that Haman died? How does the humblest man on the face of the earth end up experiencing the destruction reserved for the proud?

I Peter 2:24 gives us the answer: "He himself bore our sins in his body on the tree, that we might die to sin and live to righteousness. By his wounds you have been healed."

The humblest man on the face of the earth took all of the pride of all of God's people, and He bore it in His body on the cross. Jesus went to the cross to die the shameful death of the proud, in our place. It was our pride, our desire to be the center, our willingness to use others for our own benefit, that drove Jesus to the cross.

The cross is God's antidote to our pride. The cross is the place where Jesus takes our pride upon Himself and dies the shameful death that you and I deserve. Because of that, you and I can now die to our pride.

The cross comes to kill our pride of superiority by showing us what we really deserve. We are jealous when others get what we long for, because we think we deserve it more than they do. But the cross confronts us with the truth.

You don't deserve a girlfriend or a boyfriend; you deserve to die naked on a cross and enter an eternity of suffering under God's wrath. You don't deserve to be pregnant, you don't deserve to get a promotion at work, you don't deserve to lead, and I don't deserve a bigger church. We all deserve the cross. That's it. We are not better than other people.

The humblest man on the face of the earth took all of the pride of all of God's people, and He bore it in His body on the cross.

What would happen to your pride if you believed that? How could we go on trying to be the center, if we believed we deserved the cross? Jesus bore our pride on the cross so that we could die to the pursuit of our own glory and acknowledge that we deserve the cross. Of course, once we realize how sinful we are and that we deserve the cross, how are we supposed to avoid falling into utter despair? How are we supposed to avoid the pride of inferiority? Let's look again at I Peter 2:24 to see what Peter has to say: "He himself bore our sins in his body on the tree, that we might die to sin and live to righteousness. By his wounds you have been healed."

Jesus died the death that we deserved and thus paid for our sins. That is what the end of this verse makes clear: "By His wounds you have been healed." There is no place for despair, no place for self-pity, no place for the pride of inferiority—your God has paid the price for your sins, and now you are healed.

Pride

You are healed! You can die to your pride and live to righteousness. On the cross, our Savior literally takes our place. He takes our pride and dies our death, and then He offers us His righteousness. Jesus offers us His humility. Jesus never had to be humble: He was God, and it wouldn't have been sinful for Him to have demanded to live at the center. But if Jesus wanted to save sinners like us, then He would have to be humble for every time that we would fail. Jesus humbled Himself so that He could give us His perfect humility.

The only way we will ever stop grasping after the center is if we find Someone that we believe is more worthy of it than we are. The only way we will stop making life all about us is if we find One Who is greater than we are and choose to make life all about Him.

Hear me. Jesus is better than you. He is more worthy of the center than you. Not just because He is God, but because He has loved you and given His life on the cross for you. The reason we strive so hard for the center is that we are afraid that if we don't get it, then we will be undone. We are afraid that whoever is in the center won't take care of us.

Well, we can stop grasping after the center now, because Jesus alone is worthy of the center, and He will not forget us. In Hebrews 13:5b, Jesus says, "I will never leave you or forsake you."

So take your eyes off of yourself and look to Jesus. Let His beauty and His worth and His love overwhelm you; let His power and majesty and glory entrance you; let His kindness and mercy overwhelm you; let His promises protect you; let His resurrection from the dead give you a living hope. He is the center, and life is so much better when we realize that.

CHAPTER 9: INTERCESSION

Text: Esther 8

On that day King Ahasuerus gave to Queen
Esther the house of Haman, the enemy of the
Jews. And Mordecai came before the king, for
Esther had told what he was to her. And the king
took off his signet ring, which he had taken from
Haman, and gave it to Mordecai. And Esther set
Mordecai over the house of Haman. Then Esther
spoke again to the king. She fell at his feet and
wept and pleaded with him to avert the evil plan
of Haman the Agagite and the plot that he had
devised against the Jews.

(Esther 8:1-3)

I WANT TO TELL you the story about a woman in Rwanda
because I think it will help us better understand what is
happening in the book of Esther.

Jeanne had always liked her neighbor whose name was
Innocent.

She would run into him heading to the river to fish as she was
on her way to weed her green bean patch. In the evening, Innocent
would give Jeanne's husband Nicholas a few extra fish that he'd

caught that day, and then they'd share a few glasses of beer made from banana juice and roasted sorghum. Jeanne was always grateful for Innocent. She had eleven children, and the fish helped fill the dinner table.

In 1990, ethnic tensions that had been smoldering for years ignited. Jeanne, who was a Tutsi, remembers her Hutu neighbors saying: "The time will come when we will kill all of you. From children to unborn babies, to the elderly, we don't want any of you left behind. You will all perish."

Jeanne had to pull her kids out of school because their classmates beat them up as they walked to school in the morning. "You Tutsis are useless!" the children would yell at them.

Their Hutu neighbors stopped talking to them—even Innocent, who was a Hutu. He was never much for politics, but he seemed swept up in the fury. The tension in villages and towns around Rwanda smoldered. Then, on June 6, 1994, the plane carrying the Rwandan president was shot down. He was a Hutu, and Rwanda exploded into killing.

The neighbors started by toying with them, a dark kind of harassment.

"Everyone outside," a neighbor barked at Jeanne, Nicholas, and their eleven kids. "Make a straight line."

"Why are you doing this?" Jeanne cried out. "We're friends!"

"We can't be friends with the Tutsis, with snakes like you," they responded.

"Start praying," they said, "because you're all going to die."

But that night, they hadn't come to kill—just to terrify. They walked off into the night, leaving Jeanne and the kids trembling and confused.

"I wondered," she says, "how people could change in such a short time. How could someone turn against you who has been your friend—who you've lived with in the same neighborhood without any problem, your kids visiting each other—and all of a sudden they start calling you names and killing you?"

Nicholas wondered if their neighbors really had it in them to kill their good friends. Could Innocent, his drinking buddy, really take a machete to him? Jeanne knew he could. So she gathered up the kids, all except her two grown sons who thought they'd be fine at home, and fled to the woods.

Not long after, Innocent showed up at the family house with a machete. Jeanne doesn't know exactly what happened, but friends later recounted what they saw. She says her two oldest boys—who were funny and warm and bought pens and notebooks for their younger siblings, who had known Innocent most of their lives—tried to hide, but he found them. He found them, and he killed them with his machete, and then he walked home and told his wife what he'd done.[17]

Can you imagine for a moment what it must have been like to live as a Tutsi in Rwanda during this time? To wonder, with Nicholas, if your friends and neighbors really had it in them to kill you? To believe, like Jeanne, that they did? To know for certain like her two oldest sons, that the man who once brought you fish at night and drank with your dad was searching to kill you with a machete?

The reason I brought up this story at all is because I believe that it helps us begin to grasp what it must have been like to be

---

[17] Lane Hartill, "Love and Forgiveness After Rwanda Genocide," crs.org/Rwanda/love-and-forgiveness (unknown date).

a Jew during the time of Queen Esther. Haman, the enemy of the Jews, had sent a decree throughout the entire empire, giving explicit instructions to all the people. They were commanded, "to destroy, to kill, and to annihilate all Jews, young and old, women and children, in one day, the 13th day of the 12th month . . . and to plunder their goods" (Esther 3:13).

Could you imagine being Jewish and hearing that decree read in the streets? It would be hard enough simply being a minority; knowing that you don't fit in with everyone else; making a living working six days a week when everyone else gets to work seven.

And now everywhere you look, people are staring at you. Your neighbors that you have been friends with all your life stop talking to you. The bullies that never liked you anyway now smirk and laugh whenever they see you. You notice people walking outside your house, and you can hear them arguing about who is going to get your stuff after you are gone. You watch the way men begin to look at your daughters or your wife, and you realize that they are just waiting for the day to come when they can kill and rape everyone that you love—and pillage everything you have spent your life working for.

The Jews know that there is no escape. That is why we read in Esther 4:3b that, "wherever the king's command and his decree reached, there was great mourning among the Jews, with fasting and weeping and lamenting, and many of them lay in sackcloth and ashes."

Now it's easy for us to hear stories like this and to feel really sorry for these people, while at the same time feeling secure that nothing like this could ever happen to us.

But to do that would be a grave mistake; these stories are actually just a shadow of another day that is still to come. 1 Thessalonians 5:2 says,

> For you yourselves are fully aware that the day of the Lord will come like a thief in the night. While people are saying, "There is peace and security," then sudden destruction will come upon them as labor pains come upon a pregnant woman, and they will not escape.

Revelation 6:15-17 speaks about this day when it says,

> Then the kings of the earth and the great ones and the generals and the rich and the powerful, and everyone, slave and free, hid themselves in the caves and among the rocks of the mountains, calling to the mountains and rocks, "Fall on us and hide us from the face of him who is seated on the throne, and from the wrath of the Lamb, for the great day of their wrath has come, and who can stand?"

The Bible is radically clear that a day is approaching when God will come and judge all of His enemies. On that day, God will bring His justice with Him. He will come and search for all those who have rejected Him as King; He will find them and sentence them to eternal suffering.

Jonathan Edwards describes hell like this:

The devils in hell will hate all of the damned souls there. They hated them while in this world and that is why they sought their ruin through their subtle temptations. They thirsted for the blood of their souls, because they hated them; they longed to get them in their power to torment them; they watched them as a roaring lion does his prey; because they hated them, therefore they flew upon their souls like hell-hounds, as soon as ever they were parted from their bodies, full of eagerness to torment them. And now that they have them in their power they will spend eternity in tormenting them with the utmost strength and cruelty that devils are capable of. They are as it were, continually and eternally tearing these poor damned souls that are in their hands. And these souls will not only be hated and tormented by devils but they will have no love or pity toward one another, and will be like devils one to another, and will, to their utmost, torment each other, being like brands in the fire, each of which helps to burn the others.[18]

The hell that is coming to all those who do not know Jesus will make the worst suffering that this world has ever seen seem light and momentary. So don't think of these stories as distant and inapplicable because they are but shadows of the judgment that each one of us was born under.

Earlier, we saw that Queen Esther, who had previously been hiding the fact that she was Jewish, courageously went before the

---

[18] Jonathan Edwards, *Charity and its Fruits* (Carlisle, PA: The Banner of Truth Trust, 2000), 360.

king and begged him to save her life and the life of her people. The king couldn't believe that someone would threaten the life of his Queen, and he demanded to know who had done such a thing. Esther pointed at Haman and said, "A foe and enemy! This wicked Haman!" The king had Haman impaled on the stake that Haman had built to impale Mordecai on. After the king killed Haman, his anger abated.

In Esther 8, we learn the aftermath of Haman's death. The king takes all of Haman's stuff and gives it to Esther. Esther tells him that she is an orphan, and that Mordecai has raised her like a daughter. The king takes the signet ring off of Haman and gives it to Mordecai and makes him the second-most powerful man in the empire. Then the king returns to his throne thinking that the matter has been settled.

The king has saved Esther's life along with the life of her family, and he has given Mordecai a powerful position; so the king assumes that will be enough for Esther. The king assumes that Esther will be satisfied with having her own life spared and having the only family she knows elevated to power. He assumes Esther will be able to forget about the fate of the rest of the Jews and simply return to living for herself. He assumes that, because that is exactly what he intends to do.

This is exactly what many of us have chosen to do, isn't it? We have put our trust in Jesus, and we have been saved from the hell that we just spoke about so that now we don't have to be afraid of death anymore. Jesus, the Son of God, has born the torments of hell that we deserved, and He has set us free. When we understand how horrible hell is and how great God's wrath is against His enemies, the fact that Jesus came and took our place ought to absolutely overwhelm us.

But now I want us to consider how we have responded to this good news. I think many of us have responded the way the king thinks Esther should respond. Knowing that we don't have to be afraid of death anymore, we have decided to get back to focusing on our work or our family or on a new relationship. Having been saved, we have returned to pursuing our own comfort and pleasure while the people all around us are still living under the threat of God's eternal judgment.

Having been saved, we have returned to pursuing our own comfort and pleasure while the people all around us are still living under the threat of God's eternal judgment.

Consider for a moment the things that seem to consume your attention each day. What are you spending your life on? Is it work? Is it raising your family? Is it worrying about what other people think about you? Is it thinking about what you will do for fun this weekend?

What do you allow to consume your thoughts and your attention each day? What if Esther had done that?

What if Esther had let figuring out how to redecorate Haman's house consume her day? What if she had let catching up with Mordecai, whom she hadn't seen in five years, consume her day? What if she let taking a break after all the stress of the last few months consume her day?

That would be crazy. Millions and millions of Jews are out there living under the imminent threat of death, and it would be absolutely crazy for her to decide that, since her life is safe, she doesn't need to worry about anyone else.

So what does Esther do? In Esther 8:3-5, we read:

> Then Esther spoke again to the king. She fell at his feet and wept and pleaded with him to avert the evil plan of Haman the Agagite and the plot that he had devised against the Jews. When the king held out the golden scepter to Esther, Esther rose and stood before the king. And she said, "If it please the king, and if I have found favor in his sight, and if the thing seems right before the king, and I am pleasing in his eyes, let an order be written to revoke the letters devised by Haman the Agagite, the son of Hammedatha, which he wrote to destroy the Jews who are in all the provinces of the king."

Esther goes on to explain why she can't just be happy for her own life. She tells the king why she can't just think about herself and pretend that everything is okay. She says, "For how can I bear to see the calamity that is coming to my people? Or how can I bear to see the destruction of my kindred?" (Esther 8:6).

Esther goes before the king and pleads with him to save her people because she can't bear to see them destroyed. She can't focus on herself, knowing that they will soon be tormented. The idea of Esther's going on with her normal life while her people are about to be destroyed is ludicrous to her. It's crazy. She can't do it.

Intercession

Every year, over 100 firefighters in America die trying to save people's lives.[19] Every year, 150 police officers in America die in the line of duty.[20] On September 11, 2001 alone, over 400 emergency workers died at the foot of the twin towers.[21] Why? These men and women risked their lives in order to try to save people who were in danger. They couldn't bear to watch someone be destroyed without doing something about it.

If even non-Christian men and women are willing to risk their lives in order to save people who are in physical danger, how much more should you and I be willing to do whatever it takes to try to save people from spiritual danger?

How is it that we can go through life focused on ourselves and on our jobs and our pleasures, when people all around us are perishing, and we have the message they so desperately need?

Horatio Bonar says it like this:

> The question, therefore, which each of us has to answer to his own conscience is, "Has it been the end of my life and ministry, has it been the desire of my heart to save the lost and guide the saved? Is it under the influence of this feeling that I continually live and walk and speak? Is it for this I pray and toil and fast and weep? Is it for this I spend and am spent, counting it, next to the salvation

---

[19] http://www.cdc.gov/niosh/fire, (January 1, 2015).

[20] http://www.nleomf.org/facts/officer-fatalities-data/year.html, (January 1, 2015).

[21] "Kennewick Commemorates 9/11," http://www.tri-cityherald.com/2014/09/11/3147937/Kennewick-commemorates-911.html, (September 11, 2014).

of my own soul, my chiefest joy to be the instrument of saving others?"[22]

Listen to how Paul talks about his desire for his people to be saved in Romans 9:1-3:

> I am speaking the truth in Christ—I am not lying; my conscience bears me witness in the Holy Spirit—that I have great sorrow and unceasing anguish in my heart. For I could wish that I myself were accursed and cut off from Christ for the sake of my brothers, my kinsmen according to the flesh.

Paul could not bear to see his people destroyed. He pled with God on their behalf. And then he gave his life to proclaiming the good news to them.

Paul knew how it was that he had been saved. He knew that he had been a persecutor of the church and that he deserved to suffer in hell for all eternity. But you see, Jesus didn't let that happen to him. Instead, Jesus loved Paul and left heaven to go to the cross and shed His precious blood so that He could save Paul. After rising from the dead, Jesus went before the Father and pled with Him on Paul's behalf. Then on the road to Damascus, Jesus appeared to him and brought him the good news that even after all he had done, Jesus' blood was big enough to save him.

If you have been saved, it is because Jesus wasn't content to live for Himself. If you have been saved, it is because Jesus refused to watch you be destroyed. He suffered and died in your place and

---

[22] Horatius Bonar, *Words to Winners of Souls* (P & R Publishing, 1995), 7.

then pled before God the Father saying, "If I have found favor in Your sight, and if You are pleased with My sacrifice, then save My people."

You and I have been saved because Jesus pled with God the Father on our behalf. In light of this, don't you think we should be a people who plead with God for others? Don't you think we should be a people who can't bear to watch the ones we love die under God's judgment? Don't you think we should be a people who refuse to live for ourselves as long as there are people going to hell?

You and I have been saved because Jesus pled with God the Father on our behalf. In light of this, don't you think we should be a people who plead with God for others?

It is immortal souls that we pass by each day; immortals headed for everlasting horror or everlasting splendor.[23] With that in mind, we have no right to live for ourselves. So won't you remember that you have been saved because Jesus pled with God on your behalf? And won't you take time to plead with God for others? Plead with Him for your family, friends, coworkers, and neighbors; plead with Him to open up doors and to give you opportunities to tell others the good news about Jesus.

Esther risked her life to plead with a king who she knew couldn't care less about the Jews, and yet he still listened to her.

---

[23] C.S. Lewis, *The Weight of Glory* (San Francisco, CA: Harper Publishing, 2001), 45-46.

You and I have free access to the King of the universe any time we want, and we know that He loves to save people. So how much more ought we to plead with Him to save those that we love?

The king hears Esther's request and gives Esther and Mordecai the freedom to write up any law they want and seal it with his seal. So Mordecai writes up a law that will be good news for all of the Jews. It frees people from feeling compelled to kill the Jews and actually warns people that if they do try to kill the Jews, they will be met with justice. The language of the law mimics the language of Haman's law to ensure that it is exact justice. Anyone who attempts to kill the Jews and their families in order to take their possessions does so at the risk of their own lives, families, and possessions.

This law is good news for the Jews. When the Jews hear this law, verse 16b tells us that they, ". . . had light and gladness and joy and honor."

But Mordecai knows that it's not enough to simply write up a law that will be good news. What would have happened if Mordecai would have simply written up a good law and then posted it on a bulletin board outside the palace? It wouldn't have been enough. For good news to work, people have to hear it.

So notice what Mordecai does. In verse 9, we see that he addresses this news to every single province in the empire, and then he has this good news translated into every single language of the empire. Specifically, he makes sure that this good news is translated into the language of the Jews; he wants them—those who have been languishing under the threat of destruction—to hear the good news in their own language. Then Mordecai sends these letters by mounted couriers riding on swift horses that were bred from the royal stud.

APPLICATION

You and I have had the tremendous privilege of receiving good news, and the question is: what are we going to do with it?

In Romans, Paul specifically addresses this issue. He begins by reminding us of the good news in Romans 10:13: "Everyone who calls on the name of the Lord will be saved." But then in verse 14 he says,

> How then will they call on him in whom they have not believed? And how are they to believe in him of whom they have never heard? And how are they to hear without someone preaching? And how are they to preach unless they are sent? As it is written, "How beautiful are the feet of those who preach the good news!"

Do you hear what Paul is saying? He is telling us that the good news which has saved us must be shared. It won't be believed unless it is shared. It's not enough to merely receive the good news. We must be a people who share it with others.

The Bible wasn't written in English. It was actually written in Greek and Hebrew and Aramaic; if it had been left that way, probably none of us reading this would be saved. But in the early 1500's, a man named William Tyndale took the good news and translated it into English. And do you know what happened to him? In 1535, he was arrested; in 1536, he was executed by strangulation, and his body was burned at the stake. But do you know what he did just before he died? He prayed, and his dying request was that God would open up the eyes of the King of England. Two years later, the eyes of the king were opened, and he authorized the English translation of the Bible so that it might be used in all of the churches of England.

Never forget that if you know Jesus today, it's because somebody translated God's word for you. It's because someone pled with God on your behalf. It's likely because someone took the time to talk to you about Jesus, to invite you to come to church, or to give you a Bible.

You have been saved from the torments of hell because other people shared with you the good news of the Gospel. Nevertheless, there are probably many people in your life who are currently on their way to eternal suffering. So let us be a people who cannot bear to watch those we love be destroyed. Let us be a people who lovingly yet boldly tell others the good news about Jesus. Don't be content to simply believe in Jesus; instead, give your life to making this good news known to others.

If you are reading this, and you still don't know Jesus, and you're trying to figure all this out, then I want you to know just how fortunate you are. I want you to know that you have someone praying for you, someone pleading with God for you. Before this book was ever started, a group of us gathered to plead with God for anyone who might read this book, who didn't yet know Jesus.

What we prayed is that God would open your eyes, that He would make it radically clear to you that you are a sinner in desperate need of being rescued; that He would help you realize the horror that you rightfully deserve and are currently headed for; that you would know that despite your sin and brokenness, there is One Who loved you and Who willingly gave His life on the cross so that you might not perish but have eternal life.

I pray that you would come to know this One Whose name is Jesus. I plead with you to receive His death on the cross for your sins as good news. I beg that you would repent of your sins and put your trust in Him and that you would know the joy and gladness that comes from experiencing Jesus' love.

When the Jews heard Mordecai's law, the Bible says that they, "had light and gladness and joy and honor." Oh my friends, that is what I want for you. That is what I want for all of us. I want us to have life and light and joy and gladness. I want us to be free. I want us to know the height and depth and breadth of Jesus' love for us (Ephesians 3:18), and I want us to be always ready to share this good news with anyone who will listen.

Chapter 10: Great Reversals

Text: Esther 9-10

Now in the twelfth month, which is the month
of Adar, on the thirteenth day of the same, when
the king's command and edict were about to be
carried out, on the very day when the enemies of
the Jews hoped to gain the mastery over them,
the reverse occurred: the Jews gained mastery
over those who hated them.

(Esther 9:1)

W E LIVE IN a broken world, and sometimes it can
be really hard to understand what God is doing:

- We say that God is good, yet so much of what happens
  in this world seems to be bad.
- We say that God is love, yet this world is full of so much
  hate.
- We say that God is in control, yet it often seems like we
  are surrounded by chaos.
- We have the Bible full of amazing promises, yet our lives
  are often filled with disappointment and heartache.

One thing is certain: if God is in control, He isn't running the universe the way we would!

That is a tension that I think all of us are very familiar with. What I have loved about Esther is that instead of hiding from this tension, instead of sugar-coating everything to make it palatable, the book of Esther actually highlights this tension. In the book of Esther, there are many times where you find yourself wondering where God is and trying to understand what He is doing.

Consider two of our major players. Where is God when

- a young orphan girl is taken into the harem of an arrogant, womanizing, power hungry, unstable, violent king?
- the great enemy of God's people, one of the most arrogant men in all the Bible, gets promoted to the second-most powerful position in the empire?

We think God opposes the proud, but it certainly looks like Haman is doing pretty well for himself. He has ten sons, a wife, wealth beyond anything we can imagine, and all this political power. All of this while Esther, one of God's own people, doesn't even have a mom or dad—and she is ripped away from the only family she knows and placed into the harem of the king.

Then Haman uses his power to make a decree that is intended to kill, destroy, and annihilate every Jew in the entire world. This decree is sent out into the entire empire, and—because it is sealed with the king's own ring—it cannot be revoked. So where is God in that? If He knows Haman is so evil, why does He ever let him have so much power?

In the middle of this book, we find that all of God's promises are being threatened, and His name hasn't even been mentioned. So where is God? And what on earth is He doing? That is the tension that permeates the early part of the book of Esther.

And because of that tension, the book of Esther is full of suspense. Each section seems to end with some sort of cliffhanger:

- Chapter 3 ends with the entire city of Susa thrown into confusion by the king's edict to destroy all the Jews.
- Chapter 4 ends with Esther agreeing to risk her life by going in to see the king. Her final message to Mordecai is, "If I perish, I perish" (Esther 4:16b).
- Chapter 5 is full of suspense:
  - When the king asks Esther what her request is, instead of telling him that she is a Jew and pleading for her life, she asks that the king come to a meal she is preparing for him.
  - When the king asks her at that meal what she wants, she puts it off for another day.
  - That night, Haman builds a 75-foot stake that he intends to hang Mordecai on early the next morning.

And then overnight, everything begins to change. Haman is forced to honor Mordecai the exact way he would like to be honored, and he ends up dying the exact way he had hoped to kill Mordecai. Mordecai is given Haman's position, and he writes a decree which allows the Jews to defend themselves.

Now it's just a matter of waiting. The enemies of the Jews plot against them, and the Jews prepare to defend themselves. Finally, the fateful day chosen by Haman's dice comes around. The author begins chapter 9 by writing, "Now in the twelfth month, which is the month of Adar, on the thirteenth day of the same, when the king's command and edict were about to be carried out . . ." (Esther 9:1a). The day has come. We wait with anticipation to see what is going to happen.

Now we expect the author to tell us this story the same way he has told the other stories in this book. We expect the suspense to build as he talks about the Jews gathering in the cities to protect themselves. We expect him to tell us about their enemies and how the battle unfolded. We expect the climactic scene in this book to carry all the drama and suspense that we have seen in all the previous chapters.

So in order to do justice to this story, I want you to read the text for yourself. You may want to hang on to your seats!

> Now in the twelfth month, which is the month of Adar, on the thirteenth day of the same, when the king's command and edict were about to be carried out, on the very day when the enemies of the Jews hoped to gain mastery over them, the reverse occurred: the Jews gained mastery over those who hated them. (Esther 9:1)

That's it! One verse, and you already know how the story ends. No suspense, no turns, no detailed descriptions. The most climactic day in the entire book is laid out in one verse. Now the author has more to tell us about this day, so he will use the next

18 verses to fill in the details; but there is no suspense in these verses. There is no real drama because he has already told us how the story ends. It's like he tells you the final score of the game before you sit down to watch it.

Why? In a book full of drama and suspense, complete with last-minute reversals, why does the author choose to take all of the drama out of the most climactic scene? Why, when everything still hangs in the balance, is the author so quick to summarize the conclusion? I think that's a question the author wants us to ask ourselves.

And I think the author has a very good reason for doing what he did. (Just so you know, I am not alone; one of my favorite commentaries on Esther agrees with me.[24])

I think that the reason the author ends the story the way he does is because the end of this story has never really been in question.

Stay with me for a second. The conclusion of this story is told without any suspense because the outcome of this story has never really been in question. Remember what Mordecai says to Esther in 4:14? He says, "If you keep silent at this time, relief and deliverance will rise for the Jews from another place . . . . And who knows whether you have not come to the kingdom for such a time as this?"

Notice that there is no question in Mordecai's mind about the outcome of this story. There is no suspense about whether or not God's people will be delivered. If you had asked Mordecai how God's people would be delivered, he would have said, "who

---

[24] Karen Jobes, *Esther* (Grand Rapids: Zondervan, 1999), 203.

knows?" Maybe God will use Esther, or maybe she will keep silent. Who knows? But one thing is certain: God will deliver His people.

The 13th day of the 12th month was always going to end the same way. It was always going to end with God's people being delivered. There has never been any suspense around that day, and that is why the author chooses to summarize it in the first verse.

You see, God had made promises to His people:

- He would be their God, and they would be His people (Jeremiah 32:36ff).
- He would gather them from all the countries to which He drove them in His anger, and He would bring them back and make them dwell in safety (Ezekiel 37:24ff).
- He would send a King to His people, from the tribe of Judah, to rescue His people and establish an eternal kingdom (II Samuel 7:1-16; Matthew 1:21).

And because of these promises, the deliverance of God's people was never really in question. This story was always going to end with God keeping all of His promises, with His people being delivered, and with His enemies being judged.

Our lives are full of drama, aren't they? Our lives are like the middle of the book of Esther where circumstances can change in the blink of an eye. One second, we are on top of the world; then, before we know it, something happens and it seems like everything is falling down around us.

I think about a pastor friend of mine who thought his 14-year-old daughter had a sinus infection; then she went in for a

CT scan, and she actually had a tumor around an artery in her brain.

I think about the family in our church that went to the beach a few years ago. They were body surfing when Bill, the father, got caught in a wave that threw him down headfirst into the ground and broke his neck. His limp body was carried from the ocean, and he was rushed to the hospital for an eleven-hour surgery. No one knew if he would be paralyzed or not. [25]

We live in a world of uncertainty, a world full of suspense, where everything can change with the blink of an eye. I recently went with my family to San Francisco, and we walked onto the Golden Gate Bridge. The day was really windy, and it was a really long way down. I don't like heights, but I wanted to look over the edge. Every time I would try, I would get really scared. I felt like my glasses and my hat were going to fly off, and—without thinking—I was going to reach for them and stretch too far and lose my balance and fall. But I really wanted to look over the edge! Finally, I found a light post that went way up in the air, and I realized if I hugged the light post, I could look over the edge.

Life sometimes feels like I felt on that bridge. It feels scary, like at any moment we could go over the edge. But I want you to know that there is a post to hold onto—the living and abiding Word of God. Just like in the book of Esther, there is no suspense about how our story will end. In the end, God wins, and He keeps all of His promises.

---

[25] In case you are wondering, my pastor friend's 14-year-old daughter had surgery to remove the tumor, but it grew back again. She has had a second surgery, and they are praying that this time the tumor doesn't return. As for Bill, his surgery was a total success, and he was walking again within months.

Great Reversals

It's true that the middle of our story may go a number of ways. In the middle of the story, sometimes God's enemies seem to have it all. In the middle of the story, sometimes God's people suffer. In the middle of our story, if someone asks us how God could possibly keep His promises, sometimes the best answer we can come up with is, "Who knows?"

We don't always understand what God is doing. We don't always know why He lets certain things happen in the middle of our stories. But Esther comes to tell us a different story. Esther reminds us that there is no suspense about how the story ends; even when the path seems uncertain, the end remains unchanged. In the end, God wins. In the end, God delivers His people. In the end, God keeps all of His promises.

However bleak things may seem, however hopeless they appear, however impossible they look, the book of Esther has shown us that our God is the God of great reversals. He is the God who turns things upside down in a moment.

In a matter of seconds, Haman goes from being the second-most powerful man in the empire to being impaled on a stake in his own backyard. Mordecai goes from certain death to wearing the king's robes. God's people go from mourning, fasting, weeping, and lamenting in Esther 4:3 to, "light and gladness and joy and honor," in Esther 8:15.

Now what this teaches us is that because our God is the God of great reversals, we simply cannot judge things by the way they appear right now. That is a truth that God longed for His people to remember. In order to help them remember this truth, Esther and Mordecai declare the 14th and 15th day of the 12th month to be an annual feast.

162

Esther 9:27-28 says,

> The Jews firmly obligated themselves and their offspring
> and all who joined them, that without fail they would
> keep these two days according to what was written and
> at the time appointed every year, that these days should
> be remembered and kept throughout every generation.

During this feast, the Jews would read the entire book of
Esther out loud. This would remind them that even when you
can't see where God is, you can always know what He is doing.
Even when you don't understand why things are going the way
they are, you can know that He is working everything in the
universe together in order to keep His promises.

---

*God is able to take even the darkest days and
use them for good.*

They called this feast Purim, named after the dice (Pur) that
Haman had cast in order to crush and destroy the Jews. Even the
name of this feast is meant to remind God's people of the great
reversal. One of the songs that they would sing at this feast says,
"All the world was struck with amazement, when Haman's Pur
became our Purim." They wanted to remember that God was able
to take even the darkest days and use them for good. He is able
to take the very day that Haman sought to destroy the Jews and
use it to bring them relief from their enemies. He is able to take
a day of sorrow and turn it into a day of feasting.

The feast of Purim is meant to give God's people hope in their darkest days. It is meant to remind them that there is no drama about how the story ends. It is meant to remind them that even when everything seems out of control, even when it seems like God has abandoned them, even when it looks like their enemies will get mastery over them, they can trust God because the end is certain. That is the message of Purim, and that is the message that God never wants His people to forget.

Do you know why He didn't want them to forget this message? It's because He knew that there was a really dark day coming, a day where no one would understand what He was doing.

God knew that a day was coming when the Messiah Who was supposed to rescue His people and set up His kingdom would be put on trial and sentenced to death and hung upon a Roman cross. God knew that when that happened, the sun would refuse to shine, and the world would be covered in darkness. He knew that His own Son would cry out to Him and say, "My God, my God, why have you forsaken me?" (Matthew 27:46b). And even though everyone there would wait in anticipation to see what happened, God knew that they wouldn't hear an answer.

God knew that from within that story, it would look like

- He had abandoned His only Son.
- He was failing to keep His promises.
- God's enemies had gained mastery over Him.

He knew this, and that's why He instituted the feast of Purim in Esther's day. He wanted His people hundreds of years after

Esther to remember that He was the God of great reversals. He instituted Purim so that even on their darkest days—on Jesus' darkest day—His people could know that they could trust Him. He wanted them to remember that no matter what happens in the middle of the story, the end is certain. God wins, and He keeps all of His promises.

The disciples forgot about Purim. They forgot how the story ended. They forgot that their God was the God of great reversals, and so they judged Him by their present circumstances. That is why their hearts were filled with sorrow, and their minds were overwhelmed with fear, and they ran and hid in a locked room. They thought the story was over. When Jesus hung His head in death, they thought that was the end.

But on that dark day, there was One Who didn't forget about Purim. There was One Who never lost sight of how the story ended. Even though He was forsaken in the middle of the story; even though God didn't answer His cry for help in the middle of the story; even though His suffering exceeded anything this world had ever known in the middle of the story—this One refused to judge God based on His present circumstances.

I Peter 2:23 says, "When he was reviled, he did not revile in return; when he suffered, he did not threaten, but continued entrusting himself to Him who judges justly." In Luke, we find that His last words from the cross were not, "My God, my God, why have you forsaken me?" (Matthew 27:46b). No, his last words were, "Father, into your hands I commit my spirit!" (Luke 23:46b).

Jesus remembered the lesson of Purim. He remembered that his Father was the God of great reversals. He refused to judge God based on the middle of the story, so He was faithful even unto death. With the world black, with the weight of all His people's sin resting upon His shoulders, with the wrath of His Father pouring down upon Him, Jesus never gave up hope. Amidst it all, He never forgot how the story ended. He never forgot that in the end, God wins. Hanging from that cross, Jesus never forgot that in the end, God would deliver all of His people. Jesus never forgot the truths of Purim, and that is why He was able to remain faithful unto death.

And do you know what? Jesus was right. He was right because against all odds, God came through and kept all of His promises.

God did not abandon His Son to Hades, nor did He let His holy One see corruption (Acts 2:31). Instead, on the third day, the God of great reversals rolled away the stone and raised His only Son from the dead just like He had promised.

Not only did God raise Jesus from the dead, but Philippians 2:9-11 tells us that,

> Therefore God has highly exalted him and bestowed on him the name that is above every name, so that at the name of Jesus every knee should bow, in heaven and on earth and under the earth, and every tongue confess that Jesus Christ is Lord, to the glory of God the Father.

That is how the story ends, and Jesus never forgot that. He knew that His Father was the God of great reversals. He knew that on the very day that His enemies thought they were gaining mastery over Him, the reverse would occur, and God would gain mastery over all of His enemies. That is why Hebrews 12:2b says, "Who for the joy that was set before him endured the cross."

Purim was meant to be a shadow of the cross. At the cross:

- Satan plotted against Jesus to crush and destroy Him. But when it came before the King, He gave orders that the evil plan Satan had devised against Jesus would return on his own head. Colossians 2:15 tells us that at the cross, "[God] disarmed the rulers and authorities and put them to open shame, by triumphing over them in [Jesus]."
- The day that Satan sought to destroy God's only Son became the day that God's people received relief from all their enemies.
- Jesus conquered sin and death and hell, disarmed the accuser, and set His people free.

APPLICATION

Today, we may not celebrate Purim anymore, but that is only because we have a better feast meant to celebrate an even better victory. That is what communion (the Lord's Supper) is meant to do. You may wonder why most Christians partake of the Lord's Supper on a regular basis. Let me give you just a few reasons:

- To celebrate how God brought us relief from our enemies.
- To celebrate that our sins have been forgiven.
- To celebrate that death has been conquered.
- To remember that God always keeps His promises.
- To remember that He will never leave us or forsake us.
- To remember that there is no greater love than the love that Jesus has already poured out upon His people.

- To remember that we can't judge God in the middle of the story because our God is the God of great reversals:
  - The death of Jesus that looked to His original disciples like defeat, has been transformed into something that we celebrate.
  - What was once the darkest Friday in the history of the world, we now call Good Friday.
  - What the disciples thought was the last supper is something we now celebrate as the Lord's Supper.

You and I need communion because we need to be reminded about how the story ends. We need to be reminded that in the end, God wins and keeps all of His promises.

So please don't judge God by your present circumstances. Don't let the middle of the story confuse you. Don't let the prosperity of the wicked or the suffering of God's people throw you off. Instead, look back to the cross and know that our God is the God of great reversals. He is the God Who is able to fix even the most broken situations. He is the God Who raises the dead. And even when you don't understand what He is doing, you can know for certain that he has a plan. Even when you don't see Him, you can be sure that He is there.

Remember that in the entire book of Esther, the name of God isn't mentioned once; yet in the face of overwhelming odds, every single one of God's promises is kept. You don't have to see God for Him to keep His promises; you don't have to understand His path to know where it will end. The story ends with God's rescuing His people and crushing His enemies.

There is simply no suspense about that. The only question is, whose side will you be on when the curtain falls? All of us must choose a side. All of us trust in something. What will you put your trust in? Will you trust yourself, even though you know you're not really in control? Will you trust your feelings, even though they have deceived you in the past? Will you trust your present circumstances even though they can change in the blink of an eye?

If you haven't put your trust in Jesus, I am begging you to trust Him. If the book of Esther has taught us anything, it's that we can trust God. Even if the book of Esther isn't enough, certainly the cross ought to be enough, shouldn't it? Why would you doubt a God Who loved you enough to shed His blood on the cross in your place? Why would you doubt a God who was strong enough to raise His Son from the dead? Why would you let something horrible in your life right now cause you to doubt God when you have seen that our God is the God of great reversals? His light shines in the darkness; He fixes broken things; He is able to raise the dead.

If you have put your trust in Jesus, then the next time you take communion, I want you to take your eyes off of your circumstances and remember how the story ends. Let go of trying to control everything, and remember that the God Who did not spare His only Son is going to keep all of His promises to you. Trust God. I promise you, no one who puts their trust in Him will ever be put to shame.

Appendix: Holy War

The Jews struck all their enemies with the sword,
killing and destroying them, and did as they
pleased to those who hated them. In Susa the
citadel itself the Jews killed and destroyed 500
men, and also . . . the ten sons of Haman the son
of Hammedatha, the enemy of the Jews, but they
laid no hand on the plunder.

(Esther 9:5-6, 10)

I N THE BIBLE we read about God:

- sending a flood to destroy the entire world.
- pouring down fire on entire cities.
- calling Israel to destroy whole nations in the land of
  Canaan.

For many people—Christians and non-Christians alike—there
seems to be a tension that exists when we read about God's wrath
and judgment in the Old Testament, and then Jesus' love and
forgiveness in the New Testament. In the Old Testament, God

fights with Israel against their enemies, while in the New Testament, God calls us to love our enemies. For many people, this tension is enough to keep them from believing in God; for others, it's just confusing, and they try to read through these passages as quickly as possible.

My goal in this appendix is to try to alleviate some of that tension and answer some questions, even if we can't get to all of them here.

In Esther 9, the Jews are attacked by a people who hate them. Earlier in the story, Haman the Agagite, the enemy of the Jews, writes a decree calling everyone in the Persian Empire to destroy, kill, and annihilate all of the Jews they know—young and old, women and children. However, before that terrible day comes, Haman is executed, and a Jewish man named Mordecai takes his place.

Even though Mordecai can't change Haman's decree, Mordecai makes another decree that allows the Jews to defend themselves against anyone who comes and tries to kill them. Finally the day comes, and Esther 9:1b-2 says,

> On the very day when the enemies of the Jews hoped to gain the mastery over them, the reverse occurred: the Jews gained mastery over those who hated them. The Jews gathered in their cities throughout all the provinces of King Ahasuerus to lay hands on those who sought their harm. And no one could stand against them.

In verses 5-6, we read,

The Jews struck all their enemies with the sword, killing and destroying them, and did as they pleased to those who hated them. In Susa the citadel itself the Jews killed and destroyed 500 men.

In verse 16a, we read,

Now the rest of the Jews who were in the king's provinces also gathered to defend their lives, and got relief from their enemies and killed 75,000 of those who hated them . . . .

All of this is done in self-defense. The Jews gather together and only fight against people who hate them and are trying to kill them, destroy their entire families, and take all of their possessions.

Have you ever watched one of those horrible scenes in a movie where men with machine guns come down on a village in Africa and start lining people up and shooting them and killing the kids and raping the women and pouring gas on everything and burning it? Let's say you are watching a movie like that, and there are some other soldiers just outside the village. What would you want the soldiers to do? You would want them to go down there and kill the men with the machine guns, right? You would want them to stop the rape and murder. You would probably cheer if they killed the leader who was going from village to village, killing and burning everything in his sight.

That is what is happening in the story of Esther. The only people who die in this story are people who have armed themselves and attacked the Jews in order to wipe their entire race off the face of the earth and take all of their stuff. After the day is over, the King asks Esther what she wants; in verse 13b, she says, "If it please the king, let the Jews who are in Susa be allowed tomorrow also to do according to this day's edict. And let the ten sons of Haman be hanged on the gallows."

Esther who used to be so sweet and compliant now asks the king for another day for the Jews to defend themselves against their enemies. She knows that there are people who still really want to kill all the Jews, and she wants to give her people one more day to defend themselves against them and so get rid of the people who hate them. She also wants Haman's sons to be treated like God's enemies and hung on a tree. In the law of the Jews, it says, "Cursed is everyone who is hanged upon a tree" (Galatians 3:13b). Esther wants people to see that Haman and his entire family who have tried so hard to destroy God's people are under God's curse.

I want to give you a little bit of background on what we see happening here in Esther, but I also want to use this opportunity to talk a little bit about Holy War in the Bible and how it fits in with the God of the New Testament, Who tells us to love our enemies.

First, a little bit of Old Testament history. Haman, the enemy of the Jews, is from the tribe of Amalek. The Amalekites are the first people to attack Israel after they have been rescued from Egypt. When Israel is a brand new nation, right after they have been rescued from Egypt and are wandering in the desert, the Amalekites come and attack them and try to kill them all and take their stuff. Sound familiar?

In Exodus 17, God gives Israel victory over the Amalekites and then says to Moses in 17:14, "Write this as a memorial in a book and recite it in the ears of Joshua, that I will utterly blot out the memory of Amalek from under heaven."

God judges Amalek for attacking His people, and His judgment is that He will destroy even the memory of Amalek.

Later, Saul becomes the first king of Israel, and God sends him on a mission to utterly destroy the Amalekites—to destroy them completely, in order to fulfill the promise God made to Moses.

Now this idea of destroying an entire people from the face of the earth is one that is really difficult for us to understand, isn't it? Today, when one nation tries to completely get rid of another nation, we call it genocide and recognize that it is absolutely evil. So how is it possible for God to call Saul to destroy all the Amalekites?

The name that we give to this kind of war is Holy War, and it was different than any other kind of war. Here are some things that distinguished Holy War:

- Holy War wasn't decided by a king in a palace or by a general or by a vote; it was commanded directly by God.
- In Holy War, Israel wasn't allowed to keep any of the spoils; everything was to be devoted to destruction, and anything that wasn't destroyed was put in God's treasury.

In Holy War, Israel was simply being used by God to bring judgment on His enemies; that is why they weren't allowed to profit from the war by taking spoils. In this sense, Holy War should be seen just like the flood or just like God sending fire on Sodom and Gomorrah.

Now that we have rightly understood this kind of war as God's judgment on His enemies, we have to ask:

WHAT GIVES GOD THE RIGHT TO DESTROY A WHOLE CITY OR A WHOLE TRIBE?

How does this God Who sends judgment on entire cities mesh with the God we read about in the New Testament?

I think one of the reasons we find it so offensive to hear about God's destroying an entire city is that we assume that people are basically good and have the right to live. All we hear is the name of a tribe that is destroyed, and we picture these innocent people going about their own business completely unaware of what is about to hit them.

But that isn't the case. The Amalekites are our first example. When they saw two million former slaves wandering in the desert, thirsty and looking for water, remember what they did? They gathered up an army of men and tried to wipe Israel off the face of the earth and take all of their stuff.

And it's not even like this is just one bad generation of mean people. From then on, the Amalekites are continually trying to raid Israel's villages and take their stuff. When Saul comes to power, God calls him to put an end to the Amalekites so that His people might have peace. But Saul doesn't do it. In fact, Saul decides to let one of the Amalekites live.

The name of the man he let live: Agag. Hundreds of years later, one of Agag's descendants—Haman—does exactly what his people have tried to do from the beginning: wipe the Jews off the face of the earth and take all of their stuff.

Every time you see God exercise His wrath and judgment in the Old Testament, it is important to remember that the people deserve it.

The Canaanites are our second example. In Deuteronomy 9:3, Moses says,

> Know therefore today that he who goes over before you as a consuming fire is the LORD your God. He will destroy them and subdue them before you. So you shall drive them out and make them perish quickly, as the LORD has promised you.

So here, God is telling Israel that He is going to go before them and judge their enemies and thrust them out before them. He goes on in verse 4 to make it clear that the Canaanites deserve this punishment because of their wickedness.

Moses writes in Deuteronomy 9:4-5:

> Do not say in your heart, after the LORD your God has thrust them out before you, "It is because of my righteousness that the LORD has brought me in to possess this land," whereas it is because of the wickedness of these nations that the LORD is driving them out before you. Not because of your righteousness or the uprightness of your heart are you going in to possess their land, but because of the wickedness of these nations the LORD your God is driving them out from before you, and that

he may confirm the word that the LORD swore to your fathers, to Abraham, to Isaac, and to Jacob.

Why does God drive out the Canaanites? Because of their wickedness. Because they deserved it. The Canaanites are not good people. The Canaanites hate God, and they perform human sacrifices on their kids, slitting their throats and offering them up on altars to idols that they have made out of wood and stone.

God has given the Canaanites 400 years to repent. For 400 years, God has left his people enslaved in Egypt so that He can give the Canaanites time to repent of their wickedness. Generation after generation, God waits; but they won't stop. They won't stop killing their kids and worshiping idols and doing sorcery and rejecting the God Who made them and gave them everything that they have.

The God of the Old Testament isn't a wrathful God Who flies off the handle and loves to kill His enemies; He is a patient God Who is slow to anger but Who will eventually enact justice on people who refuse to repent. Deuteronomy 7:9-10 says:

> Know therefore that the LORD your God is God, the faithful God who keeps covenant and steadfast love with those who love him and keep his commandments, to a thousand generations, and repays to their face those who hate him, by destroying them. He will not be slack with one who hates him. He will repay him to his face.

My friends, when you read about people being destroyed in the Old Testament, you can know that they were people who hated God. God wants us to know that He will not tolerate being hated forever. One day, He will come and repay everyone who rejects Him and has chosen to live their lives as His enemy.

So, the reason God pours out His wrath on people in the Old Testament is because they deserve it. However, in Deuteronomy 9:6-7, Moses says,

> Know, therefore, that the LORD your God is not giving you this good land to possess because of your righteousness, for you are a stubborn people. Remember and do not forget how you provoked the LORD your God to wrath in the wilderness. From the day you came out of the land of Egypt until you came to this place, you have been rebellious against the LORD.

The reason God punishes the Canaanites is because of their wickedness; yet this passage makes it pretty clear that the people of Israel aren't any better. Instead, even after everything God does to rescue them, they remain stubborn and rebellious.

So this passage leaves us with another sort of tension. Do you see how this passage has forced us to change the question? The question is no longer, "How can God destroy the Canaanites?" That answer is pretty straightforward: they hate God, and He repays them by giving them the justice they deserve. That answer works for every person in the Bible that God ever destroys.

The real question that this text exposes is:

Appendix: Holy War

HOW CAN GOD BE SO KIND TO ISRAEL EVEN THOUGH THEY ARE SUCH A REBELLIOUS PEOPLE?

The Bible tells us that in the beginning, God creates everything that exists. He makes Man and Woman in His image; He plants them a garden and walks with them each day and gives them everything they need.

He gives them a world of peace, a world without death or pain or suffering. He gives them all sorts of food to eat. He gives them a perfect relationship with each other so that they are naked and not ashamed. He gives them all of this, and yet they want more.

There is one tree in the entire garden that God has said to them, "In the day that you eat of it, you shall surely die" (Genesis 2:17). But they rebel against God and reject His word; they eat of the one tree in the whole garden that God has forbidden them to eat from. In doing, so they reject God and declare that the perfect world which He had made for them isn't enough.

At that moment, the story should be over. At that moment, God should come in His wrath and destroy Adam and Eve.

But He doesn't kill them like they deserve, and from that moment on, a massive tension begins. It isn't about how God can be so cruel, but about how He can be so kind. It isn't about how He destroys His enemies, but about how He can let His enemies live. From that moment on, the question becomes, "How can God be just and still allow sinners like Adam and Eve and all of their children after them to live?"

You and I and every person that has ever lived are alive because God chose to be gracious to Adam. And yet even though God chose to be gracious to Adam, every single human being who has ever been born has been born with Adam's same heart of rebellion against God. That is why the Bible is so clear in Romans that, "There is none is righteous, no, not one; no one understands; no one seeks for God. All have turned aside; together they have become worthless; no one does good, not even one" (Romans 3:10-12).

Just as Haman followed in the footsteps of his father Agag, and Haman's sons followed in his footsteps, so all of us have chosen to follow in the footsteps of our father Adam. Because of that, Romans 6:23 makes it really clear that we deserve death. It says, "The wages of sin is death." Everyone who has ever sinned deserves death.

When we read the Bible like this, the tension should overwhelm us. It's not the judgment and death in the Old Testament that should surprise us; it's the life that permeates every single page that is so surprising.

How is it possible that God allowed Adam and Eve to live? How does He let Cain live after he murders his brother Abel? Why does He give the Canaanites 400 years to repent before He finally sends Israel to take their land? Why does He give the land to Israel anyway, since they are a stubborn and rebellious people?

What gives God the right to let people live when the wages of sin is death? What gives God the right to lavish people with good gifts when the law says, "Cursed is everyone who does not abide by all things written in the book of the law" (Galatians 3:10b)? How can God make so many good promises to such bad people?

Appendix: Holy War

The Bible is about a God Who makes precious and very great promises to people who don't deserve them. Look what God promises:

- Life to people who deserve death
- Heaven to people who deserve hell
- Love to people who deserve wrath
- Joy to people who deserve sorrow
- Peace to people who deserve warfare
- Grace to people who deserve justice

How can God make such great promises to a people who don't deserve them? That is the tension in the book of Esther.

That is the tension that I will try to alleviate for you. You see, there is one time in the Bible where God does destroy an innocent Person; one time when God wages Holy War against Someone Who does not deserve it.

This person is born of a woman, but He isn't a son of Adam. This man is born of a virgin, and He is the very Son of God. This innocent man lives the perfect life that all of us have failed to live. Because of that, He deserves all of the promises of God. Because of His righteousness, He deserves life and heaven and love and peace and joy. Yet He experiences death and hell and wrath and warfare and sorrow. This innocent man is treated like the worst of criminals. This Son of God is hung on a tree as if He were the son of one of God's worst enemies.

The Holy War that God executed on the Canaanites is what God should have poured out on Adam, along with each one of us the first time we sinned. Instead, God sent His only Son, Jesus;

Jesus took all of the sins of all of God's people on Himself, and then He let God wage Holy War against our sin in His body while He hung on the cross (I Peter 2:24).

Isaiah 53:10 tells us, "It was the will of the LORD to crush him; he has put him to grief." Isaiah 53:5-6 tells us,

> But he was wounded for our transgressions; he was crushed for our iniquities; upon him was the chastisement that brought us peace, and with his stripes we are healed. All we like sheep have gone astray; we have turned—every one—to his own way.

And because of that, we deserve God's wrath; but Isaiah 53:6b says, "And the LORD has laid on him the iniquity of us all."

On the cross, God crushed His only Son for the sins of His people. He consumed Him as He had once consumed the Canaanites; He judged him like He had judged Sodom and Gomorrah; He repaid Him for all of the times that we have rejected God. God poured out the ultimate judgment that we deserved for our sins on His only Son.

He did that so He could reconcile His enemies to Himself. Paul says it like this:

> Since, therefore, we have now been justified by his [Jesus] blood, much more shall we be saved by him from the wrath of God. For if while we were enemies we were reconciled to God by the death of his Son, much more, now that we are reconciled, shall we be saved by his life. (Romans 5:9-10)

Appendix: Holy War

CONCLUSION

The tension in the Bible has never been why the God of the Old Testament poured out His wrath on His enemies after giving them 400 years to repent. It has never been why He sent the flood on a people whose wickedness was great and whose every intention and thought was evil continually.

The tension in the Bible is found in God's precious and very great promises that He makes to sinners, when what they really deserve is His judgment. The tension is found when the innocent Son of God hangs on a cross; it comes when He cries out to His Father, "My God, my God why have you forsaken me!" and there is no answer.

The answer to that tension is that we have a God Who loves His enemies and has graciously sacrificed His only Son so that whosoever would believe in Him might not perish but have everlasting life (John 3:16).

So how should we respond to this God? If you have put your trust in Jesus and have been saved from the just wrath of God, your only response can be one of worship. Let the judgments that God poured out on His enemies in the Old Testament remind you of what you have been saved from. Let it point you to all that your Savior bore for you on the cross. You and I were enemies of God, but He loved us and sent His Son to rescue us; then He pursued us until our eyes were open and we realized just how amazing He is. That is a God worth worshiping.

This news should move us not only to worship, but also to love our enemies. When we realize that we were once enemies of God who have only been saved because He loved us, then we will be able to love our enemies in the hope that God will come and

184

rescue them as well. As long as we feel we are better than our enemies, we will want justice for them; but when we realize that we are just as bad as our enemies, and the only difference is that God has been gracious to us, then and only then will we be able to have compassion on our enemies.

You see, right now, God is being patient with His enemies. Right now, God is holding back His wrath in order to give people an opportunity to turn to Jesus and experience His mercy and forgiveness. We must never forget that it was God's patience with us that saved us. As long as God continues to give people life, we must love them and long for them to be reconciled to God.

If you don't yet know Jesus, I beg you to come to Him and experience His love and forgiveness. All of the judgments of God that we see poured out in the Bible are just foretastes of the end-times judgment that He will one day pour out on all of His enemies. II Thessalonians 1:7 tells us that when the Lord Jesus is revealed from heaven with His mighty angels in flaming fire, He will inflict vengeance on those who do not know God and on those who do not obey the gospel of the Lord Jesus Christ.

Right now, God is being patient with His enemies. He is giving you an opportunity to repent. He has shown you how serious He is about sin, and now He is pleading with you to come to Him so that He can forgive you of all your sins and rescue you from the hell that you deserve.

What a patient God we have! What a loving God we have! But don't presume upon His kindness. Romans 2:4-5 says,

> Or do you presume on the riches of his kindness and forbearance and patience, not knowing that God's

kindness is meant to lead you to repentance? But because of your hard and impenitent heart you are storing up wrath for yourself on the day of wrath when God's righteous judgment will be revealed.

Let us not be a people who presume upon the kindness of our God. He has graciously given us glimpses of His wrath in the Bible so that we wouldn't presume upon His kindness but instead would repent and turn to Him. Let us be a repenting and rejoicing people; a people who recognize our sin and see God's kindness to us and are quick to repent and plead with Him for mercy; a people that receive His mercy with thanksgiving and are quick to give Him praise for the way that He has loved us and given His life to rescue us and adopt us into His eternal family.

That is what our God is like, and He is worthy of our worship.

Timothy Cain (M.A. Westminster Theological Seminary) is the lead pastor of Kaleo Church which he planted in El Cajon, California, in 2009. Kaleo Church is a part of the Treasuring Christ Together (TCT) Church Planting Network. Tim has a passion for preaching the Gospel, church planting, adoption, and feasting with the poor. He and his wife Abbey live in El Cajon with their two adopted children.

Made in the USA
Coppell, TX
17 December 2019